Ethics of Responsibility

WALTER S. WURZBURGER

Ethics of Responsibility

PLURALISTIC APPROACHES
TO COVENANTAL ETHICS

The Jewish Publication Society
Philadelphia & Jerusalem
5754   1994

Manufactured in the United States of America

LIBRARY OF CONGRESS CATALOGING-IN-PUBLICATION DATA

Wurzburger, Walter S.
     Ethics of responsibility : pluralistic approaches to covenantal ethics / Walter
S. Wurzburger. — 1st ed.
       p.   cm.
     Includes bibliographical references and index.
     ISBN 0-8276-0514-5
     1. Ethics, Jewish.   2. Orthodox Judaism — Doctrines.   I. Title.
   BJ1285.W87   1994
   296.3′85 — dc20   93-47414
                                                                              CIP

DESIGNED BY MARTHA FARLOW
TYPESET IN GALLIARD BY GRAPHIC COMPOSITION, INC.

To NAOMI

The publication of this volume was made possible in part by a grant from ROCHELLE and EDWARD BERKOWITZ.

A person's entire life must not be conducted on the basis of exclusive reliance upon a single trait.

— Saadiah Gaon, *The Book of Beliefs and Opinions*

The commandments were given only in order to ennoble creatures.

— Leviticus Rabbah, 13:3

Contents

CONTENTS

Preface & Acknowledgments

THIS BOOK GREW OUT OF MANY YEARS OF STUDY-ing, writing, and lecturing on ethical issues. My revered teacher, Rabbi Joseph B. Soloveitchik, inspired me to treat Halakhah not merely as a legal system but as the matrix of ideas, concepts, and values of fundamental importance to Jewish philosophy. Although I have frequently referred to Rabbi Solo-veitchik in this book, it is impossible to adequately record my indebtedness to him.

I also want to acknowledge my gratitude to Professor Isadore Twersky, whose seminal works have provided me with important insights into the Maimonidean approach to law and philosophy.

Dr. Norman Lamm, president of Yeshiva University, has earned my gratitude for suggesting that I write a book on Jewish ethics. My students at Yeshiva University, where I have been teaching courses for many years both in Jewish and general ethics, have been a source of challenge and stimulation to me.

My thanks go to the Memorial Foundation for Jewish Culture for providing me with a grant for the research leading to the publication of this book.

Some of the ideas in this book originally appeared in my writings in various journals and scholarly publications. I thank Yeshiva University Press, Spertus College of Judaica Press, Kluwer

Academic Publishers, and *Tradition* for permission to republish material from my writings.

Since much of this work deals with Maimonides, it was especially helpful that New York University Press granted me permission to use the translations that appear in the *Ethical Writings of Maimonides,* by Raymond L. Weiss, with Charles E. Butterworth. Unless otherwise indicated, translations from Hebraic and Aramaic sources are my own. Scriptural texts, however, are cited from the Bible translation of The Jewish Publication Society.

I am especially fortunate that Dr. Ellen Frankel, editor-in-chief of The Jewish Publication Society, has advised and guided me in revising the original manuscript. Her editorial and literary skills contributed not merely to the readability of the book but also led me to clarify what otherwise might have remained obscure.

My friend, Professor William Kluback, has read many sections of the manuscript. I have benefited enormously from his wisdom as well as from his invaluable stylistic suggestions.

Above all, I want to thank my beloved Naomi, to whom this book is dedicated, for being a model of an "ethics of responsibility." Paraphrasing what Rabbi Akiva said of his wife, "Whatever contribution I may have made is really hers."

WALTER S. WURZBURGER

LAWRENCE, NEW YORK

ELUL, 5752

Ethics of Responsibility

Introduction

I T IS GENERALLY ASSUMED THAT TRADITIONAL JU-
daism constitutes a purely legalistic religion that revolves
exclusively around obedience to Halakhah (religious law).
In this book, I hope to dispel this misconception and demonstrate that Jewish piety involves more than meticulous adher-
ence to the various rules and norms of religious law; it also demands the cultivation of an ethical personality.

From my perspective, Halakhah represents not merely "the
way *of* God"—that is, a divinely revealed body of laws; it also
functions as a way *to* God, leading not necessarily to mystical
union with Him, but to a life dedicated to responding to Him
through obedience to His commandments and imitation of His
ways. I believe that, based upon Maimonides' interpretation of
the biblical text, the verse "thou shalt walk in His ways"[1] chal-
lenges us to cultivate an "ethics of responsibility."[2] More is required than mere compliance with the explicit rules prescribed
by Halakhah. We are commanded to engage in a never-ending
quest for moral perfection, which transcends the requirements
of an "ethics of obedience."

It is no coincidence that ethics plays such a pre-eminent role
in the Jewish conception of piety. Pagan cults separated ethics
and religion and regarded the performance of various cultic rites

as the hallmark of religion. They looked upon their deities solely as ultimate powers controlling the forces of nature. In the pre-scientific era human beings could do very little to harness the forces of nature to their purposes. The primitive mind resorted to rites and sacrifices in hope of swaying the gods to respond to human needs.

Jewish monotheism represents a radically different approach to religion. Its novelty consisted not primarily in the substitution of the belief in one God for the plurality of gods worshiped in polytheism. What was even more revolutionary in the Jewish conception of monotheism was, as against the pagan emphasis upon divine power, the attribution of moral perfection to God.

His moral attributes rather than His absolute power render Him *worthy* of being worshiped and obeyed. In striking contrast to paganism, worship is no longer dictated primarily by self-serving considerations as a device enabling us to get what we want. To serve Him is not a means to the fulfillment of our needs, but an end in itself. Worship of God involves commitment to abide by His will and the ethical norms He demands.

For many years, I have attempted in a number of papers to demonstrate that intuitive ethical beliefs play a central role in the halakhic system,[3] which seeks to provide normative guidance for living in conformity to the will of God. In this book I develop my thesis systematically and show that the continuous interaction between ethical intuitions and formal legal elements in halakhic Judaism generates a distinctive Jewish ethics.

As opposed to numerous strict constructionists,[4] I contend that the halakhic system serves merely as the foundation of Jewish piety, from which arises what I term "Covenantal Ethics." In the latter, intuitive ethical judgments play a major role. But it must be emphasized that Jewish ethics is theocentric. Its authority is not based upon human autonomy but upon the belief that our ethical intuitions reveal to us divine imperatives stemming from our Covenantal relationship with God. As opposed to modern Jewish thinkers who, under Kant's influence, contend that religion is a postulate of ethics, I maintain that Jewish ethics is derived from religion and not the reverse.

Covenantal Ethics is based upon a variety of specific, independent norms such as prohibitions against murder, theft, adultery, perjury, and so forth. It eschews any kind of reductionism, making no attempt to explain its various prescriptions by reference to a single criterion. Only by a process of induction from particular instances may we gradually extrapolate several general principles.[5]

The pluralism of Jewish ethics manifests itself in the readiness to operate with a number of independent ethical norms and principles such as concern for love, justice, truth, and peace. Since they frequently give rise to conflicting obligations, it becomes necessary to rely upon intuitive judgments to resolve the conflict. There is, however, another dimension to the pluralism of Jewish ethics: it is multi-tiered and comprises many strands. It contains not only objective components such as duties and obligations, but also numerous values and ideals possessing only subjective validity. Moreover, the pluralistic thrust of Jewish ethics makes it possible to recognize the legitimacy of many alternate ethical values and ideals.

I must emphasize, before proceeding with a more detailed exposition of my views, that, unlike many prominent Jewish ethicists, I am approaching this subject from a traditional Jewish perspective, accepting Halakhah as the supreme normative authority. For me, Halakhah represents the revealed will of God. The positions of classical Reform as well as of Conservative Judaism and Reconstructionism are the very antitheses of my approach. For them, the promptings of the autonomous human conscience constitute the highest court of appeals in all ethical matters.

It is, however, one thing to affirm that God demands moral conduct and that since He is morally perfect His commandments are necessarily morally perfect. It is another thing to maintain — as many non-Orthodox theologians do — that if commandments do not conform to our ethical intuitions, they

could not possibly have been commanded by God. Our understanding of what is ethically required is inadequate to challenge
an explicit command of the supreme moral Authority Whose
commandments are of necessity ethically correct. Once Halakhah is acknowledged to be "the word of God"—that is, the
highest possible moral authority—deviations from its norms
cannot be sanctioned, even when halakhic norms run counter to
the perceived dictates of the human conscience.

My belief in the supernatural Revelation of the Torah also pre-
vents me from equating Judaism with the affirmation of "ethical
monotheism." In the classical sources of Judaism, the divine
summons for Israel to form a "holy people" calls for compliance
not merely with universalistic ethical norms but also for a special
concern for the role of the Jewish people, to whom a host of
particularistic ritualistic ordinances are addressed.

My conception of Halakhah differs sharply and radically from
that espoused by modern Covenantal theologians,[6] who have
adopted Franz Rosenzweig's doctrine of Revelation. Although
they reject Martin Buber's antinomian conclusions, they nevertheless share Buber's aversion to belief in any form of supernatural communication of content between God and man. For
them, as for Rosenzweig, Revelation amounts merely to a
"Revelation of Presence." Within this theological framework,
Halakhah is reduced to a human response to a divine Revelation
of Presence.

With the belief in *Torah min ha'shamayim* (Divine Revelation
both of the Written and the Oral Torah), Halakhah represents a
system both of supernaturally revealed teachings and divinely
ordained canons of interpretation. The Torah is, therefore,
viewed not as a purely human effort to reach out for transcen-
dence, but as the record of God's will for Israel.

I make no claim for the infallibility of any specific interpretation of the Torah. Human beings cannot pretend to be in possession of absolute truth. The binding authority of the Halakhah
does not rest upon the claim that the interpretations provided
by the properly constituted authorities of any specific historical
period reflect the only possible proper interpretation of the will

of God. What makes the Halakhah authoritative is the belief that, although there are numerous possible interpretations of the Torah, we are supposed to follow for normative purposes the decisions reflecting the majority opinion of the competent scholars of one's time. According to the self-understanding of the Rabbinic mind, scholars of the Law are charged with the responsibility of ascertaining the meaning of the Divine Revelation by recourse to the methods and procedures that are deemed appropriate for the elucidation of Torah texts. Torah "is not in Heaven."[7] Israel is not merely the passive recipient of divine teachings, but a partner with God in the creation of the Oral Torah.

My thesis that there is a uniquely Jewish ethics would not be tenable within the framework of an ethics that adopts rationality, maximization of pleasure, or, for that matter, any other evaluative criterion that is advanced as universally valid. Were I to adopt such an ethical position, I could, at the very most, argue that an ethics could be constructed (to borrow Hermann Cohen's phrase) "out of the sources of Judaism."

In the light of modern developments in ethical theory, my claim that there is a distinctly Jewish ethics has become much more plausible. Ever since Nietzsche, the doctrine of a universally valid, objective ethics has been widely challenged. The popularity of ethical theories such as "emotivism" and "prescriptivism" indicates that there is no longer any kind of consensus that ethics can be grounded either on reason or on nature. I find myself in substantial agreement with Bernard Williams's view that, since ethics relates to the domain of the "ought" and not to that of the "is," ethical beliefs cannot be based upon empirically verifiable facts.[8] All ethical reasoning, therefore, must ultimately rest upon intuitive ethical judgments. It is to be expected that an ethics formed within the matrix of a halakhic system will differ from the kind of ethical judgments that reflect the societal norms of a secular culture.

The fact that Covenantal Ethics operates with intuitions that represent value judgments arising from specific historic-cultural situations does not weaken its claim to universal validity. Moral judgments invariably express the beliefs of particular individuals. This does not imply that they are perceived as possessing only subjective or relativistic relevance. On the contrary, it is the very nature of every moral judgment that what is intuited as a moral *obligation* is immediately perceived as universally valid and applicable to every conceivable agent.

The applicability of the norms and values of Jewish Covenantal Ethics is by no means restricted to the members of the Jewish Covenantal Community. Although at the present time the religiously committed Jewish community seems to turn ever more inward and tends to focus primarily upon the particularistic and nationalistic elements of its heritage, I believe it to be of special importance to call attention to its universalistic components. While the ritualistic elements of Judaism are completely particularistic and intended exclusively for individuals who either by birth or by conversion qualify as members of the People of the Covenant, Jewish ethical teachings are not subject to the same kind of limitation but are viewed as possessing universal relevance.

I hope that this book will evoke more than parochial Jewish interest and will contribute to the clarification of some of the perplexing moral issues of our time.

CHAPTER ONE

Foundations of Covenantal Ethics

T HE JEWISH CONCEPTION OF PIETY PLACES SPE-
cial emphasis upon ethical conduct.[1] The Torah defines
"the way of God" as the "doing of righteousness and justice."[2] One is made acutely aware of the primacy of the ethical
dimension in the Torah's account of the legislation promulgated
at Marah. Even before Israel entered into the Sinaitic Covenant,
there was need for laws governing interpersonal relations.[3]

So pronounced is the emphasis upon the ethical dimension
in the writings of the latter prophets that the term "prophetic
Judaism" was coined to describe the kind of Judaism that revolved around universal moral norms.[4] Although the prophets
were also vitally concerned with the observance of rituals, they
found it necessary to focus upon the ethical dimension of religious piety, because it was so frequently disregarded by their
contemporaries. In the post-biblical era, classical exponents of
Rabbinic Judaism such as Hillel and Rabbi Akiva viewed moral
imperatives as the very essence of the entire Torah.[5] It therefore
is not surprising that many modern Jewish thinkers such as
S. D. Luzzatto, Moritz Lazarus, Hermann Cohen, Ahad Ha'am,
and Emmanuel Levinas singled out the ethical dimension as the
very hallmark of the Jewish spirit.

A number of halakhic provisions attest to the primacy of the ethical in normative Judaism. When the performance of a ritual or cultic act involves the transgression of an ethical norm, the fact that the violation was motivated by the desire to perform a religiously meritorious act cannot be invoked as a mitigating factor in diminishing guilt. On the contrary, the Sages declare that in such a case the performance of the mitzvah, far from compensating for the moral infraction, is in itself converted into an outright sin.[6] Similarly, when an individual recites a blessing prior to the consumption of illegitimately obtained food, the blessing is in itself transformed into an act of blasphemy.[7]

Although all *ritual* commandments (with the exception of the prohibition of idolatry), including even the observance of the Sabbath[8] — the very cornerstone of Judaism — are set aside when necessary for the preservation of life,[9] *ethical* laws are in a different category. Murder or acts of sexual immorality or idolatry may not be committed even if the perpetration of these crimes is deemed indispensable to the saving of one's life.[10] According to a talmudic opinion, "it is preferable to throw oneself into a burning furnace rather than embarrass another person publicly."[11] There is a question whether one may violate someone else's property rights to save one's life.[12] Under such circumstances most authorities sanction the use of someone else's property provided that there is intent to make proper restitution.[13] There is, however, disagreement whether one may subject another human being (excluding an aggressor) to pain or injury in the attempt to preserve one's own life.[14]

It is no accident but a necessary corollary of Jewish monotheism that the hierarchy of Jewish religious values accords such pre-eminence to ethical conduct. Jewish monotheism affirms that God is the Source of all being and value. In sharp contrast to paganism, which worships deities solely as the powers in control of nature, Jewish monotheism attributes moral perfection to the omnipotent God, Who necessarily desires the good. There can be no proper worship of God without obedience to ethical imperatives.

As opposed to paganism and pantheism, the God of monotheism completely transcends nature. He is the Creator, the Source of what is and what ought to be. In the realm of the *is,* God's will generates the laws of nature, which all creatures necessarily "obey." But in the realm of the *ought,* God is the Author of prescriptive rather than descriptive laws. Unlike the laws of nature, the moral law does not create facts but establishes norms or standards governing the spiritual realm. Created in the image of God, human beings are endowed with freedom and have the capacity to choose whether to obey or disobey these laws.

Notwithstanding the differences between descriptive and prescriptive laws, both laws are grounded in the omnibenevolent will of God. The link between the real world of nature (the *is*) and the ideal world of ethics (the *ought*) is expressed in Psalm 19. After proclaiming that "The heavens declare the glory of God . . . ," the Psalmist turns to the normative sphere and continues with "The law of the Lord is perfect, restoring the soul."[15]

The Talmud goes so far as to declare that the Torah served as the blueprint for the creation of the world.[16] Natural law theories base ethical norms on the facts of nature. The talmudic doctrine reverses the order and asserts that nature is so constituted as to make possible the realization of the divine purposes (the *ought*).

The radical dichotomy between God and His creation divests nature of all sanctity. Desacrilized nature can serve neither as an object of worship nor as the source of moral imperatives. What ought to be, what is valuable or desirable, what is right or good, cannot be determined by what *is.* As Hume declared, "from 'is' to 'ought' there is no inference." The right and the good are not a function of purely natural factors (be they, as for Aristotle, purposes immanent in nature or, as in the modern world, purely subjective human desires). Value is not determined—as in current naturalistic theories—by what human beings actually value, but by the purposes of God, the Author both of what is and what ought to be, Who determines what is *worthy* of being valued.

But it is one thing to divest nature of sanctity and another to sanction irresponsible conduct toward nature. There is no justification to the accusation that the ecological crisis has its roots in attitudes engendered by the biblical doctrine that gives humanity dominion over the world of nature. The Bible cannot be blamed for the damage caused to the environment by irresponsible employment of technology. The charge "fill the earth and subdue it" (Genesis 1:28) is counterbalanced in the next chapter with the observation that Adam was placed in the Garden of Eden "to work it and guard it."[17] This implies that human beings are responsible not to nature but to God for proper stewardship of resources placed at their disposal. Although the bulk of ethical commandments address themselves to interpersonal relationships, the Torah also contains many laws designed to protect the animal world from unnecessary pain[18] or extinction[19] and to prevent the wanton destruction of fruit trees.[20]

I

Many provisions of the Halakhah clearly fall within the purview of ethics. Yet it is, nonetheless, questionable whether we are really justified in speaking of a "Jewish ethics." After all, in Leviticus such a fundamental ethical norm as "Love thy neighbor as thyself"[21] is subsumed, together with numerous ritual laws, under the overall precept of "Ye shall be holy."[22] As far as the Torah is concerned, no distinction is made between ritual and ethical laws. They form a seamless whole, indispensable for the becoming of a "holy people." Characteristically, the concluding prayer on Yom Kippur states that this sacred day was ordained "so that we may cease the oppression of our hands and return to Thee to perform the commands of Thy will." Immoral conduct emerges as the prototype of all sin. Human beings belong to God.[23] Any transgression of a divine command, whether it is ritual or ethical in nature, amounts to an infringement of the proprietary rights of God, the Creator[24] and the Owner of the universe.

This doctrine, which in modern philosophy is attributed to

John Locke, is actually anticipated already in classical Jewish thought.[25] According to the Talmud, failure to pronounce a blessing before deriving enjoyment from an object is construed as misappropriation of God's property, because there is no acknowledgment that the object used was a gift from God, to which we have no claim or entitlement.[26] Even when there is no outright transgression of a divine command, failure to adequately develop our ethical potential constitutes dereliction of our duties to our Master and Owner.[27] The notion that there is an outright *ethical* obligation to obey all divine commandments is one of the central features of Saadiah Gaon's philosophy. He argued that it is rationally demonstrable that the universe cannot be eternal, it must have had a beginning in time, and therefore there must be a divine Creator, Whose commandments must be obeyed. Many Jewish philosophers, however, accept belief in Creation only as an article of faith but not as a rationally demonstrable proposition. For them, obedience to divine commandments is a purely *religious* requirement mandated by divine Revelation.

A number of eminent thinkers contend that, since Halakhah functions as the sole normative authority of Judaism, there can be no such entity as Jewish ethics, in the literal sense of the term.[28] They maintain that ethical norms mandated by the tradition derive their prescriptive force not from their content but solely from the fact that they represent divine imperatives.[29] Support for this thesis can be found in the well-known comment of R. Ovadiah Bertinoro that the tractate *Avot* begins with the statement "Moses received the Torah from Sinai" in order to make it clear that the ethical teachings contained in this tractate do not represent ordinary human ethical insights but are ultimately based upon Revelation.[30]

Even the proponents of this view admit that *mitzvot* (commandments) can be classified as (1) *bein adam la-Makom* (between a human being and God), (2) *bein adam le-chavero* (between human beings), and (3) *bein adam le-atzmo* (involving obligations to oneself).[31] They insist, however, that the latter two *mitzvot* no less than the first one derive their normative authority solely from the property of being commanded (directly or indirectly) by God, the same as the various ritual commandments that are obeyed solely because they are divine commandments, for which no rational reasons can be provided by the human mind. From this perspective, ethical imperatives possess religious significance only if they reflect explicit halakhic requirements. Otherwise, ethical considerations are dismissed as religiously irrelevant.

In radical opposition to this view, I shall attempt to show that Judaism in fact transcends such narrow legalism and, for all its theocentric orientation and emphasis upon obedience to the Law, it endows moral judgments with genuine religious import. I employ the term "Covenantal Ethics" to describe my approach, which seeks to reconcile unconditional acceptance of Halakhah as the supreme normative authority with the recognition that our intuitive moral judgments, even when they cannot be grounded in explicit provisions of the Halakhah, possess religious significance.

Because the Law plays such a predominant role within Judaism, it is necessary to guard against likely misunderstandings of the term "Covenantal Ethics." Although "Covenant" usually is associated with contractual arrangements stipulating performance or non-performance of specific actions, it must be emphasized that the term "Covenantal Ethics" is not intended in a legalistic or parajudicial sense. After all, the Bible records a variety of covenants that do not mandate obedience to specific norms but establish a unique relationship between God and man. For all its centrality and theological primacy, the Sinaitic Covenant merely supplements but does not supersede, suspend, or invalidate any previous or subsequent covenants.

As Rabbi Joseph B. Soloveitchik has repeatedly pointed out, Jewish piety expresses itself not merely in unconditional obedience to the legal provisions of the Torah as stipulated by the Sinaitic Covenant, but also in commitment to the ideals and values that are grounded in the Covenant with Abraham.[32] The latter, which at times is also called "The Covenant with the Patriarchs," mandates (1) experiencing a sense of kinship and solidarity with fellow Jews with whom we share a common "Covenant of Fate" as well as the awareness of a singular spiritual destiny and value system,[33] and (2) acknowledging the unique and pre-eminent position of the Land of Israel as the central arena for the fulfillment of Jewish destiny. It should also be noted that, at times, Rabbi Soloveitchik expanded his analysis of the meaning of the Covenant with Abraham to include in it the additional extra-legal requirement (3) to strive for religious experiences, in which God is encountered.[34]

I look upon Halakhah as an indispensable component but not as coextensive with the full range and scope of the Jewish normative system. I deliberately avoid the term "Halakhic Ethics," preferring to speak of "Covenantal Ethics." In my view, Jewish ethics encompasses not only outright halakhic rules governing the area of morality, but also *intuitive* moral responses arising from the Covenantal relationship with God, which provides the matrix for forming ethical ideals not necessarily patterned after legal models. To use Erich Fromm's terminology,[35] Judaism provides for an "ethics of responsibility" as well as for an "ethics of duty" or an "ethics of obedience."

There is no basis for the claim once made by a prominent Christian theologian that "Judaism recognizes no religious requirement unless one can find through ingenious interpretation of the Law the necessary rules of conduct."[36] The absurdity of this characterization becomes evident when we recall the well-known talmudic statement that the verse "In all thy ways thou shalt acknowledge Him"[37] represents the most succinct formulation of our religious ideal.[38] Similarly, R. Yosei declared that "all your actions should be performed for the sake of God."[39] Acts need not be perceived as instances of a specific religious norm in order to be performed for the sake of Heaven.

The fact that every moral obligation is perceived as a religious imperative, however, does not imply that the meaning of every moral statement must be translated into a statement about what is "willed or commanded by God." For example, both an atheist and a theist may share the belief that murder is wrong, but it is only the theist who associates the characteristic of being contrary to the Will of God with the characteristic of wrongness. As G. E. Moore pointed out, the meaning of "it is good" is not synonymous with "it is approved by God," notwithstanding the fact that for the theist only what is approved by God can in point of fact be good.[40]

While some may insist that for theological ethics the statement "x is good" has no meaning other than "x is approved, willed, or required by God," such a reductionist position would make it impossible for a theist to argue with an atheist or agnostic about any ethical issue, such as the propriety of abortion. Obviously, from the perspective of the nonbeliever, any statement about divine approval does not make sense. Unless we grant that moral terms have an independent meaning completely unrelated to divine approval, there would be no common universe of discourse in which moral arguments between theists and atheists or other avowed secularists could take place.[41] The mere fact that theists and atheists employ such terms as 'good,' 'right,' 'just,' and so forth, when arguing about moral issues shows that they take it for granted that the meaning of these moral terms does not presuppose any reference to the will of God.

It should also be pointed out that, were we to treat the term 'good' as synonymous with 'being commanded by God,' the entire enterprise of *ta'amei ha-mitzvot* (providing reasons for divine commandments) would be an exercise in futility.[42] The very fact that we seek to explain divine imperatives in terms of values demonstrates that the meaning of a value term such as 'good' or 'right' cannot be reduced to the property of being commanded or willed by God. If the latter were the case, whenever we state that because a particular divine imperative possesses certain properties it is good or right, we would be merely asserting the trivial tautology that the divine imperative is commanded by God. For that matter, if all value terms such as good and right had to be analyzed into terms involving divine approval or disapproval, the distinction between rational and purely revelational commandments, which plays an important role both in Rabbinic literature and medieval Jewish philosophy, would be completely untenable.

The conception of theocentric ethics advocated here is fully compatible with the Platonic thesis set forth in the *Euthryplo*: what makes an action or motive right or good is not the fact that it is commanded by God. On the contrary, it is commanded by God because it is right or good.

I take issue with G. E. Moore's view that the "Open Question Argument" constitutes a refutation of all theological ethics. Moore argues that upon hearing "X is approved or commanded by God," one still can meaningfully raise the question, "Is x good?"[43] In answer to Moore, one can argue that once God is defined as the perfectly good Being, it follows by logical necessity that whatever is commanded by Him must be good. Thus the entire argument against theological ethics collapses.

The eminent historian Yehezkel Kaufmann already called attention to the fact that for Judaism the property of being commanded by God does not constitute the defining characteristic of moral goodness. In his words, "The Bible itself recognizes the existence of a universal moral law from primeval times, to which all men are subject."[44] This represents a re-statement of the classic formulation of Rav Nissim Gaon, who stated in his Introduction to the Babylonian Talmud that "those commandments which depend upon reason or the understanding of the heart were operative from the very creation of man"[45] and therefore in no way depended upon a special Revelation to Israel. In a similar vein, he as well as many other authorities maintains that the Noahide Laws need not be derived from Divine Revelation but fall under the rubric of commandments that are certifiable by recourse to our rational faculties.[46] Whether and to what extent medieval Jewish thinkers operated with a doctrine of natural law has been the subject of extensive scholarly debate in recent years.[47] Especially significant is the fact that Rav Kook, throughout his writings, harps upon the theme that the "ethics of holiness" does not replace or negate the minimal requirements of "natural ethics," but, on the contrary, supplements and enlarges the scope and range of ethical obligations and ideals. Hence, whatever is perceived as a moral imperative must be obeyed, even if the particular moral demand cannot be based upon explicit Jewish religious sources.[48]

It is commonly accepted that Rav Kook's position has been influenced by the thesis of Judah Loew Ben Bezalel (commonly known as the Maharal Mi-Prag), who contended that the entire domain of *derekh eretz* (social conventions) comes under the purview of reason rather than of Revelation. Although Judah Loew strenuously objects to the Maimonidean doctrine that moral laws reflect purely utilitarian considerations of societal well-being,[49] he maintains that the dictates of *derekh eretz* represent rules and conventions that make possible *yishuv* — the functioning of *civilized* society. Unlike Maimonides, who interpreted the term *yishuv* as a reference to *yishuv ha'olam* (the settlement of the world), Judah Loew defines *yishuv* as what is befitting human beings by virtue of their status as rational rather than purely natural creatures. For Judah Loew, *derekh eretz* represents the sum of the requirements for rendering the earth habitable for civilized living.[50]

Yet, even if we insist that for theological ethics the term 'good' is not translatable into 'being commanded by God,' the problem remains whether a theocentric system can make room for purely ethical considerations. One might contend that for the religious believer, there is only one criterion: being willed by God. Hence, for such a person the ethical imperative commands authority only because it is willed by God. This being the case, compliance with an ethical norm because it is commanded by God would in no way differ from compliance with a ritual law, which is likewise obeyed not because of its intrinsic properties but because it is legislated by God.

Some Jewish thinkers, even though they acknowledge the validity of an autonomous ethics, nonetheless maintain that one should comply with an ethical norm out of a desire to submit to the Divine Will rather than to satisfy an ethical requirement. To cite an especially telling example, Rabbi Baruch Epstein, writing in his *Arukh Ha-Shulchan,* emphasizes that, despite the

fact that human reason can apprehend and validate filial obligations as moral duties, a religious believer should fulfill them not
because of their intrinsic ethical merits discernible by human
reason or sentiment, but out of obedience to a divine imperative.[51] In a similar vein, R. Joseph Albo states that even those
obligations that are understood as requirements of natural law
will acquire added spiritual significance whenever they are fulfilled for religious rather than merely prudential reasons.[52]

To be sure, the belief that an ethical norm should be obeyed
in response to a divine imperative rather than for purely ethical
reasons by no means detracts from the intrinsic moral character
of the norm itself. Judaism demands total commitment to the
service of God. Every action, be it self-regarding or other-
regarding, be it inspired by self-interest or ethical concerns, ideally "should be performed for the sake of God."[53]

It may be argued that this type of theocentric orientation results in a state of affairs where the intrinsic ethical properties
of our norms become totally irrelevant, since ethical duties are
performed solely as religious obligations. But to affirm the primacy of the religious dimension does not entail the repudiation
of moral authority. Since for Judaism God represents the highest
possible moral authority, obedience to His command is not
merely a religious but also a moral requirement.

This explains why Judaism has no need for the Kierkegaardian
doctrine of "the suspension of the ethical," which demands that
whenever moral imperatives clash with religious commandments, we must subordinate our ethical concerns to the higher
authority of the religious. Once God is defined as the supreme
moral authority, obedience to divine imperatives emerges as the
highest *ethical* duty. Thus, Abraham's readiness to sacrifice Isaac
cannot be invoked as a paradigm of the "suspension of the ethical." On the contrary, it was a perfectly *moral* act. Abraham does
not cringe before the absolute power of a demon, but rather
obeys the command of the supreme moral authority.[54]

Those operating with a consequentialist ethics (for example,
utilitarianism or eudaemonism) should not find it difficult to
explain why the divine command to sacrifice Isaac was supposed

to override the general prohibition against killing. Compliance with the demands of the highest possible moral authority, which combines omnibenevolence with omniscience, is bound to lead to the best possible consequences, even in situations where divine imperatives clash with our ordinary ethical rules that generally bring about the greatest good. Obedience to an omniscient and omnibenevolent God must, by definition, yield the greatest possible good, even if our limited intellectual capacities prevent us from seeing how and why certain divine imperatives engender the most desirable consequences.

For that matter, unless couched in rigid Kantian terms, even deontological (ethics of duty) conceptions of ethics acknowledge obedience to a divine imperative as the highest *moral* requirement. Obviously, it is a *moral* duty to obey the commands of the supreme moral authority. Kierkegaard had no choice but to fall back upon the "suspension of the ethical," because he adopted a strictly Kantian position on the nature of ethics. Viewed from this perspective, even an explicit command of God cannot render an act of killing moral. Accordingly, the sacrifice of Isaac would represent the height of immorality. Abraham renounces all considerations of ethics and rationality and surrenders his son as an offering on the altar in an "absurd" submission to the Will of God. It was this "suspension of the ethical" that was the hallmark of Kierkegaard's "knight of faith."

The Kantian notion that killing, even if commanded by the highest moral authority, violates the categorical imperative seems rather strange. Kant himself maintains that in certain cases — for example, the execution of a murderer by the properly constituted authorities of the state — taking the life of an individual is not murder but a moral duty. Would it not be plausible that obedience to the explicit instructions of the highest moral authority be treated as a supreme duty,[55] which overrides all other moral obligations? Following R. M. Hare,[56] who in his ethical theory synthesizes Kantian and utilitarian elements, general ethical rules represent merely tentative intuitions, which are subject to the scrutiny of our critical intelligence. Obviously, in determining what is truly moral, the prescriptions of an omniscient and omnibenevolent God should override those deriving from our more limited intelligence.

II

We are still left with the question: if an act is moral because it possesses certain intrinsic qualities rather than because it was commanded by God, is it possible to speak of a Jewish ethics? As long as we maintain that there are objective grounds for ethical beliefs, there can be no difference between Jewish and any other ethics. Regardless of whether we adopt an Aristotelian metaphysical, a Kantian rationalistic, or a naturalistic, utilitarian approach to ethics, does it make sense to assert that Jewish Covenantal Ethics possesses features that are not shared by other ethical systems? It is highly significant that Ahad Ha'am claimed that the essence of Judaism resides in a unique approach to ethics. To demonstrate his thesis, he intended to write a comprehensive treatise on Jewish ethics. But he was forced to abandon this project because he was unable to show that Jewish ethics actually constituted a phenomenon *sui generis*.

To be sure, traditional Jews would not be disturbed if there were no distinctly Jewish ethics and if one concluded that in the ethical sphere the Torah merely mandated only universally valid norms. As opposed to classical Reform with its universalistic bias, for traditionalists the case for Jewish particularism does not rest upon a special "Jewish genius" for ethics, but revolves around the doctrine of the "Chosen People," who are obligated to observe, in addition to universal ethical laws, numerous ritual laws addressed exclusively to them.[57] It was only when Reform Judaism challenged the ongoing validity of the ritual law as not conforming to "the spirit of the time" that it felt compelled to justify Jewish particularism on the ground that Jews allegedly possessed a unique approach to ethics. Prior to this development, in periods when the binding authority of the ritual laws was taken for granted, Jewish thinkers did not hesitate to divide the Torah into universally applicable rational laws and purely revelational laws that were exclusively addressed to the Jewish people. Michael Wyschogrod has even argued that it is precisely because the ethical domain is so universal that in some Orthodox circles there is a deplorable failure to recognize that ethics represents a vital ingredient of Jewish piety.[58]

We shall return to the subject in chapter four and examine at greater length the question whether and to what extent Jewish ethical norms coincide with what are regarded as universally valid prescriptions. At this point it must be emphasized that as long as one subscribes to the notion that ethical statements are objectively true or false, religion really has nothing to contribute to the content of ethics. Its sole function in the realm of morality would be to provide additional sanctions, motives, and incentives to inspire obedience to ethical norms. It, then, would be as nonsensical to speak of a Jewish ethics as it would be to refer to a Jewish mathematics or a Jewish chemistry. Were the Jewish moral code merely to prescribe what objectively is morally right or good, then the Covenantal basis of ethical norms would have no bearing upon their meaning, validity, or significance.

Recent developments in ethics have combined to undermine the claim that there is an objective foundation (be it reason or nature) for ethical beliefs. During most of the nineteenth century, most ethical debate revolved around differences among utilitarianism, Kantian rationalism, metaphysical ethics, cultural relativism, and historicism. The argument was over which of these competing ethical theories was correct. Today it is a matter of controversy whether any ethical belief or theory can be characterized as true or false.

Starting with Nietzsche, existentialists have claimed that ethical values reflect purely subjective decisions. In their view, ethical principles are not discovered but invented. Logical positivism has gone so far as to deny any cognitive significance to ethical beliefs, since unlike scientific beliefs they are not verifiable by empirical methods. In the contemporary world, ethics has come under the sway of emotivism and prescriptivism, which has engendered an ethical relativism, bordering on outright nihilism. It is widely accepted that ethics cannot qualify as an objective normative science based upon reason or nature. Instead, ethical beliefs are regarded as being founded upon intuitive judgments as to what is right or wrong, good or evil, desirable or undesirable. Inevitably, such intuitions reflect the influence of a host of social, cultural, historical, and psychological factors.[59]

It is, therefore, to be expected that the ethical perceptions of traditional Jews who have been conditioned by exposure to Jewish values frequently diverge from the perceptions of those whose ethical sensitivities have been formed within different cultures and societies. Maimonides already pointed out that the deeply ingrained sense of pity and compassion and the resulting aversion to cruelty that is so characteristic of Jews can be traced back to the impact both of the teachings of the Torah and of various historic experiences that engendered these character traits.[60]

The belief that ethics must ultimately operate with culturally conditioned intuitions need not necessarily lead to historicism, relativism, or scepticism. It is one thing to state that knowledge of moral principles is influenced by historical or cultural contingencies, and another to maintain that there are no objectively true principles, because all morality is merely the product of human invention. The fact that our moral beliefs may be incorrect, because they are perceived through the prism of our cultural and historic situation, must not be confused with the thesis that moral judgments are purely relative to a given historical situation.

Spartan morality condoned exposing unfit babies to death by starvation; Jewish morality, on the other hand, forbade this practice. But when Jewish morality condemns infanticide, it does not simply address itself to individuals or groups committed to Jewish conceptions of morality, but it regards the Spartan conception of morality as wrong for everybody, regardless of historical contingencies. Subjectivism or cultural relativism fails to do justice to the moral experience, since moral perceptions are seen as universally applicable, without regard to the cultural or social background of the agent whose conduct is evaluated. The fact that there are moral disagreements that reflect cultural differences and that cannot be resolved on the basis of rational arguments has no bearing upon the fact that all parties to the dispute advance their moral perceptions as objectively valid and binding for all rational agents.

Because divine imperatives serve as its foundation, Jewish ethics need not address the question as to why moral norms possess a privileged status that distinguishes them from other norms. Modern philosophers often debate why considerations of morality should override various other intellectual or aesthetic values. Kant took it for granted that the autonomous moral law *qua* law commands supreme respect. But, as G. E. Anscombe has shown,[61] any kind of law-ethics patterned after the Kantian model fails to take account of a fundamental logical flaw. Once the element of a divine legislator is eliminated, reverence for the law is bound to be diminished. With the benefit of hindsight we can treat the Kantian notion that law commands respect as a mere "survival" from an era when law was based upon a transcendent source.

Equally unsatisfactory is the utilitarian approach to justifying the primacy of the ethical *ought* over other values. As H. A. Prichard has demonstrated,[62] it is by no means self-evident that we ought to strive for the greatest possible good. The notion of *ought* is simply not reducible to value terms. The very meaning of an absolute unconditional demand addressed to human beings, as opposed to a purely prudential requirement, points, as Martin Buber suggests, to a religious dimension.[63]

From the vantage point of Jewish Covenantal Ethics, the entire problem as to why ethical imperatives override all other considerations completely disappears. The moral *ought* is absolute, because a divine command constitutes, by definition, the ultimate normative standard. From a traditional Jewish point of view, it is precisely because moral norms are grounded in divine imperatives that they present themselves authoritatively and demand unconditional obedience.[64]

III

Most modern systems of ethics, such as utilitarianism, intuitionism, and Kantian formalism, rely on a single property from which specific norms are deduced.[65] Jewish Covenantal Ethics is pluralistic and reverses the process. Its points of departure are a variety of specific norms such as prohibitions against murder, perjury, robbery, or fraud. General ethical principles are secondary. They are derived by extrapolation from these norms. To argue that broad general principles provide the matrix for the specific rules underlying Jewish ethics would put the cart before the horse. As Stuart Hampshire has shown, our actual moral experience cannot be fitted into the straitjacket of ethical monism.[66]

In Jewish ethics an explicit legal norm always takes precedence over a general moral principle, even if the latter seems to reflect the general thrust of the legislation of the Torah. A telling illustration is provided by the limitations imposed upon the range of applicability of *kevod ha'beriot* (concern for the dignity of individuals). According to talmudic law, scholars were exempt from the obligation to pick up a lost article and return it to its original owner, whenever such an action would involve labors that were so much beneath their dignity that they would not perform them even to reclaim their own property.[67] The Rabbis regarded this case as a precedent justifying the suspension of laws on grounds of considerations involving *kevod ha'-beriot*. Similarly, a High Priest is prohibited from attending funerals even of his closest relatives so as to avoid contact with a corpse and the consequent ritual impurity. Nevertheless, he must personally bury a *met mitzvah* (an abandoned corpse). The Rabbis pointed to these cases to demonstrate the overriding importance of *kevod ha'beriot* and declared, "Concern for human dignity is so great that it takes precedence over a prohibition of the Torah."[68] Despite the paramount importance attached to this fundamental moral principle, the Babylonian Talmud emphasizes that the only negative precept that may legitimately be set aside on the basis of this ethical norm is the commandment mandating respect for Rabbinic authority: "Thou shalt not deviate from what they [the members of the Court] pronounce."[69] According to this view, concern for human dignity justifies the setting aside only of Rabbinic enactments (*de-rabbanan*) but not of provisions of Torah legislation (*de-oraita*) unless, as in the previously mentioned cases, the suspension is specifically mandated by the Torah itself. Thus, the Babylonian Talmud states that when an individual discovers in a public setting that he is wearing a garment that flouts the biblical prohibition against wearing *sha'atnez* (a mixture of linen and wool), he must remove it, regardless of the embarrassment suffered. It is only when the prohibition involves merely a Rabbinic extension of the biblical law that its violation is sanctioned out of concern for human dignity. In case of conflict with an explicit biblical prohibition, all other considerations must be disregarded, because "there is no wisdom nor understanding nor counsel against God."[70]

This emphasis upon obedience to the Law does not — contrary to widely held belief — reduce Jewish ethics to legalism. A trenchant observation by R. Naftali Tzvi Yehudah Berlin,[71] in a comment on the verse "Ye shall be unto Me a kingdom of priests and a holy people" (Exodus 19:6), strengthens our claim that Jewish morality transcends mere obedience to explicit rules of a legal code. R. Berlin notes that, although the Torah contains numerous specific commandments, the Sinaitic Covenant cannot dispense with the general norm "to become a holy people," because ever-changing historic realities make it impossible for any finite set of specific legal ordinances to meet the requirements of all possible contingencies.

R. Berlin's striking insight is largely responsible for my choice of the term "Covenantal Ethics." Actually, his insight represents a development of ideas already formulated by medieval Rabbinic authorities. Thus, Nachmanides states in his Commentary to Deuteronomy that the biblical passage "and thou shalt do what is right and good in the eyes of God" mandates conduct that goes beyond what is specifically prescribed in the Torah:

> First it says that you shall keep the statutes and observances which He has commanded you. Then it states that even with respect to what has not been commanded, be mindful to do the good and the right in His eyes, because He loves the good and the right. This is an important matter, because it is impossible to mention in the Torah all forms of conduct of man with his neighbors, all his business

affairs and the institutions of all civilizations. . . . After mentioning a good many of them, such as "thou shalt not slander," "thou shalt not take revenge nor bear a grudge," "thou shalt not stand idly by the blood of your fellow man," "thou shalt not curse the deaf," "thou shalt rise before the elderly," etc., then there is the general statement that "one should do the good and right" in every matter, including the need to make compromises and [to engage] in supererogatory conduct.[72]

In a similar vein, Nachmanides characterizes the Torah's methodology as proceeding by intuitive induction from particular instances to general rules.

After specifying various particular laws relating to dealings between human beings such as "thou shalt not steal," "thou shalt not rob," . . . it mentions the general rule, "thou shalt do what is right and good" to include in a positive Commandment [the practice of] righteousness, compromise, supererogation.[73]

Vidal Yom Tov of Tolosa adopts Nachmanides' approach to explain why talmudic law grants to a landowner the right of preemption of adjoining land.[74] Since no finite number of specific rules could possibly suffice to meet the requirements of all possible circumstances, the Torah, in his opinion, formulates only a relatively small number of specific moral rules that when combined with overall general principles such as "thou shalt do what is right and good" enable us to grasp intuitively the moral requirements arising from new situations. The Rabbinic enactments concerning the rights of owners of adjoining land, therefore, implement the Torah's mandate "to do what is good and right." Similarly, R. Joseph Albo declared in his *Sefer Ha-Ikkarim,*

Why was not the entire Torah given in written form? . . . [T]he law of God cannot be perfect so as to be adequate for all times, because the ever new details of human relations, their customs and their acts, are too numerous to be embraced in a book. Therefore Moses was given only certain general principles, . . . by means of which the wise men in every generation may work out the details.[75]

IV

Because mere obedience to a set of formal rules as specified by the Torah is only a necessary but not a sufficient condition of ethical propriety, another source of moral authority must be found. Nachmanides' approach, which validated the intuitions of a moral conscience formed within the matrix of Torah teachings, pointed in the direction of this authority. To be sure, such a conception of the authority of conscience differs radically from the notion that conscience can impose its own laws because it is endowed with independent, autonomous authority.[76] As Michael Walzer has put it so aptly,

> [T]he word "conscience" originally designated a kind of internal court where God's writ was thought to run, a faculty for moral judgment divinely created and implanted.[77]

Obviously, within a theocentric framework there is no room for autonomy in the literal sense of the term — that is, a human self that is self-legislating and its own source of obligation. Human beings are responsible to God rather than to themselves. To quote Micah,[78] "to do justice and to love mercy" is a response to "what God demands of thee," not a self-imposed duty. As Emil Fackenheim has pointed out, Jewish morality involves an obligation toward human beings as well as toward God.[79] Viewed from a Jewish theological perspective, the human self, far from constituting the source of moral obligation, merely apprehends what are perceived to represent transcendent norms issued by a divine Commander. Saadiah defines "rational commandments" not as self-imposed duties but as divine *commandments* that may be apprehended by our cognitive faculties and that do not require for their validation any reference to a supernatural act of Revelation.[80] Similarly, when Bahya Ibn Pakuda coins the term "duties of the heart,"[81] he refers not simply to the dictates of the human conscience but rather to divine imperatives that are apprehended by our human conscience. In the striking formulation of Meiri,[82] "the commandments perceived by the human heart are like the letters of the Torah scroll." Significantly, for all his emphasis upon the supernatural character of Judaism, Samson Raphael Hirsch also recognizes the promptings of the human conscience as a form of Revelation, contrasting the "inner Revelation" of the human conscience with the "external Revelation" that was vouchsafed to Israel at Mount Sinai.[83]

It must be emphasized that in all the above-mentioned approaches to conscience, there is no suggestion that the promptings of the conscience may be pitted against explicitly stated norms of the Torah. The Will of God represents the supreme authority to which all other considerations must be subordinated. Conscience is merely complementary to the explicitly revealed provisions of the Law; it supplements but does not supersede them. The role of conscience is limited (1) to discern the Will of God for situations that do not come within the purview of explicit legal norms and (2) to function as a hermeneutical principle to be employed to help ascertain the meaning and range of applicability of laws when their formulation contains an element of ambiguity.[84] Since the Torah is characterized in the Book of Proverbs (3:17) as "its ways are the ways of pleasantness and all its paths are peace," we should assume that, in case of doubt concerning the meaning of a divine ordinance, the interpretation that is more in accordance with our moral sensibilities was intended by the divine Legislator.[85]

Far from constituting an independent normative authority, conscience merely provides, in consonance with supernatural Revelation, an instrumentality through which the divine will may be discerned. It would be the height of arrogance to challenge the validity of an explicit divine imperative on the ground that it runs counter to our own ethical intuitions. Indeed, to permit humanistic considerations to override divinely revealed commandments amounts to a desecration of the Divine Name.[86]

In the event of conflict with explicit halakhic requirements, all ethical, aesthetic, intellectual, or prudential considerations must be set aside. Our position here is diametrically opposed to the classical Reform thesis, which rejected all ritual practices that in their opinion could not be reconciled with modern ethical sensibilities. On the contrary, the revealed word of God is the highest normative authority, which must be obeyed unconditionally and must not be subjected to the scrutiny of our autonomous moral perceptions. As noted in chapter six, there is ample provision within the halakhic process to consider a host of ethical concerns as factors in decision-making. But what matters from a theoretical point of view is that in cases where ethical considerations are perceived to clash outright with explicit and unambiguous halakhic provisions, we are duty-bound to follow in Abraham's footsteps and subordinate the promptings of our human conscience to the superior authority of divinely revealed imperatives. In the final analysis, they constitute the supreme ethico-religious standards of evaluation.

To be sure, under certain conditions Halakhah itself contains provisions enabling a court to set aside temporarily certain provisions of the Law when it is deemed necessary for the purpose of maintaining the viability of the Law itself, just as a surgeon may remove a limb if necessary to save a human life.[87] But under contemporary conditions this authority can no longer be exercised by Rabbinic authorities. Even when it was possible, temporary suspension of the Law was ordained not in order to accommodate the demands of human conscience but to make it possible to abide by other divine laws. More germane to our issue is the Rabbinic doctrine of *averah lishmah*[88] — that is, an outright transgression may be meritorious if it is motivated by the desire to serve God. But while this notion may be invoked under special circumstances to justify an individual transgression of the Law as a matter of conscience, it can by no means sanction the permanent setting aside of a law solely on the basis that it runs counter to the promptings of the autonomous conscience. As a matter of practice, the application of *averah lishmah* has been traditionally discouraged except under the most extraordinary circumstances.[89]

CHAPTER TWO

Ethical Intuitions

THE FACT THAT EXPLICIT, UNAMBIGUOUS HA-
lakhic rules take precedence over the dictates of the human conscience by no means diminishes the role of ethical intuitions in Jewish Covenantal Ethics. To begin with, there
are many areas that the formal Halakhah does not address at all
and that therefore do not come under the purview of halakhic
legislation. That religious authorities find it necessary to issue
pronouncements to their devotees as expressions of *da'at Torah*
(nonlegal but authoritative rulings of eminent Torah scholars)
rather than as outright *piskei din* (halakhic decisions) is in itself
evidence that there are religiously significant issues that cannot
be decided on the basis of purely formal halakhic reasoning.

Rabbinic authorities are frequently taken to task for their alleged failure to plumb the resources of the halakhic tradition to
extract from it authoritative prescriptions on various sensitive
political, social, or economic issues. I do not share this attitude.
Far from being disappointed that the formal Halakhah is silent
on so many questions, I am glad that Halakhah makes space for
the input of individuality and subjectivity on religiously significant issues. It should be borne in mind that meticulous observance of halakhic norms does not exhaust the meaning of Jewish
piety. Halakhah merely provides the foundation; it is a necessary

but not a sufficient condition for the attainment of religious ideals. As Rabbi Soloveitchik put it, "Halakhah is not a ceiling but a floor."[1]

In keeping with the etymology of the term, Halakhah represents only the *way*, the avenue leading to authentic, personal, religiously motivated decisions in areas that are left to the discretion of individuals. According to the Sages, one of the reasons Jerusalem was destroyed was because our ancestors merely abided by the letter of the law.[2] To properly fulfill our Covenantal obligations, it is not sufficient to satisfy the minimal requirements demanded by the Law; we must respond to an all-encompassing summons addressed to us as free individuals in our existential subjectivity, uniqueness, and particularity by God, Who is absolutely One and Unique.[3]

I

I have coined the term 'Covenantal Imperative' to denote the kind of intuitive religious responses to be given to existential situations that cannot be justified exclusively in terms of obedience to objective and formal rules of conduct. Covenantal Imperatives are not obtained by deduction or inference from legal norms but are immediately intuited as subjective religious responses to a particular concrete situation.

My conception, undoubtedly, owes much to Buber's thesis that in the "life of the Dialogue" moral requirements represent responses to a silent address by God as "directed to a specific hour of life."[4] I must, however, part company with him when he dismisses the Law as a barrier between man and God. But while I reject his antinomian approach, I nonetheless believe that some elements of his thought are extremely valuable and could be incorporated within a system based upon the primacy of Halakhah. When Buberian categories are grafted upon the structure of halakhic Judaism, one can assert that as long as a particular situation does not fall within the purview of a law, individuals should respond to the situation with what they intuit as religiously desirable.

Although this view that moral commandments, even if not

based upon any specific divine commands, represent religious requirements seems to be reminiscent of Paul Tillich's notion of "theonomy"[5] (law of God), I prefer the term 'Covenantal Imperatives.' There is no need to subsume all and sundry religious imperatives under the rubric of law, a notion that involves generality rather than uniqueness and particularity. My term 'Covenantal Imperative' is more appropriate for what is experienced as a religious requirement for a particular situation.

My commitment to Halakhah precludes my acceptance of Buber's existentialist thesis that every divine Command is addressed to a singular and unique situation.[6] But it is one thing to assert that divine commandments *can* give rise to general laws and another to claim that all divine imperatives must necessarily be couched in universal terms and engender a general law. Contrary to Kantian formalism, we may apprehend singular ethico-religious imperatives that need not be universalizable.

My conception of Covenantal Imperatives bears some resemblance to the previously mentioned doctrine of *da'at Torah,* which accords special weight to the views of eminent Torah scholars even in matters where no formal halakhic ruling is feasible. Implicit in both positions is the belief that the residual influence of exposure to halakhic categories of thought makes itself felt in areas where the law itself cannot be applied. To be sure, there is an essential difference between my conception and that of *da'at Torah.* Whereas the latter purports to represent authoritative, objective religious truth, my notion of Covenantal Imperatives disclaims any pretensions to objectivity. In my view, as long as we are dealing with matters that are not subject to halakhic legislation, there is no authoritative body to provide guidance and it is incumbent upon individuals to assume *personal* responsibility on the basis of their own purely subjective, intuitive decisions.

It should be realized that reliance upon intuitive factors is necessary not only for (1) the formation of Covenantal Imperatives to provide normative guidance for situations that do not fall within the scope of explicit formal rules. We cannot dispense with intuition even in cases (2) when we wish to subsume a particular instance under a general rule. For it is only on the basis of intuition that we can establish that a given situation is, in point of fact, an instance of the general rule. Moreover, (3) conflicting moral principles often give rise to ethical dilemmas and ambiguities. Since in many instances we do not have at our disposal formal rules specifying which of the two principles possesses greater weight, we have no choice but to rely on intuitive judgments for the resolution of many ethical dilemmas. It thus becomes clear that reliance upon intuition is indispensable, especially if we are interested in an ethics that will extend the range and scope of ethical concerns beyond the limits of sheer obedience to explicit rules so as to encompass elements that go into the makings of an ethics of responsibility.[7]

Since subjective intuitions play a significant role in Jewish Covenantal Ethics, the resulting system cannot avoid the difficulties besetting all forms of intuitionist ethics. Intuitions are notorious for their dependence upon individual idiosyncrasies, which are due to a host of genetic and environmental factors. The history of philosophy abounds with objections to reliance upon intuitions, which have been discredited as amounting to little more than purely subjective beliefs that reflect the particular psychological make-up of the individuals holding them. After all, in the days of Aristotle, it was considered self-evident that masters had the right to rule over their slaves, while we regard it as self-evident that all human beings are entitled to basic human rights. The fact that an individual is intuitively certain of the rightness of a course of action is hardly evidence of the correctness of this belief. As Justice Holmes put it, "certitude is no test of certainty."[8] The inability to imagine holding a different belief is an interesting datum about the psychological make-up of a particular person, but cannot be offered as proof of the truth of the belief.

But even though Jewish Covenantal Ethics operates with intuitions, it does not follow that the entire system must abandon all claims to objectivity. To begin with, its ultimate foundation rests upon specific moral laws that are formulated in legal terms and acknowledged as divine commandments, which override even the authority of the individual conscience. It is only in cases when we cannot have recourse to explicit formal rules for moral guidance that we must rely upon intuition. Hence, in Judaism the area in which ethical propriety is solely determined by intuition is far smaller than in ethical intuitionism. Moreover, as was noted in conjunction with the requirement to give owners of adjoining real estate preferential treatment, ethical intuitions frequently are eventually codified in the Halakhah and acquire the status of objectively binding norms, since Rabbis are vested with the authority to serve as the expositors of the meaning of the divine commandments for a given generation.

It is important to bear in mind that insistence upon moral objectivity is fully compatible with the belief that *some* ethical intuitions possess only subjective validity. Ethical ideals, in contradistinction to outright moral obligations, need not be regarded as universally applicable. There is no inconsistency in maintaining that a particular ethical ideal holds only for individuals endowed with specific traits of character or intellectual qualifications. The history of Jewish ethical thinking attests to the fact that a host of conflicting ethical ideals were advocated by individuals who acknowledged the authority of the Halakhah.

II

It thus becomes evident that Jewish Covenantal Ethics refers to a multitiered structure, encompassing a wide variety of prescriptions ranging from objectively binding moral norms to purely subjective ethical ideals. Conflicting moral obligations or competing values frequently give rise to ethical dilemmas. The pluralistic nature of Jewish ethics does not allow us to rely on a single criterion for the resolution of competing claims between various norms and values. Since there is no hierarchy of values or principles that can provide definitive guidance in situations of ethical ambiguity, we have no choice but to rely on intuition to determine which of the conflicting *prima facie* obligations takes precedence.

It should also be noted that the general principle "to do what is right and what is good" lends itself to an interpretation suggesting two distinctive ethical properties. This would be incompatible both with utilitarian and deontological approaches. The former maintain that the right is reducible to the good, while the latter point to rightness as the ultimate ethical category. But the mere fact that the Bible utilizes both rightness and goodness in its formulation of the aforementioned general principle does not really prove that the two terms are irreducible to one another.[9] It could be argued that the two terms are synonymous, especially since, according to R. Akiva's exegesis,[10] the Torah employs two distinct terms for the purpose of indicating that in addition to being right and good in the eyes of God, our actions must also have the appearance of being right and good in the eyes of others. That the Torah employs two distinct terms, therefore, indicates not the mutual irreducibility of rightness and goodness to one another, but rather the Torah's concern that we avoid not merely evil but even the appearance of evil.

Since Jewish Covenantal Ethics is composed of many strands, we cannot dispense with the utilization of our intuitive faculties in the determination of ethical propriety. For all its emphasis upon Law, Covenantal Ethics is a far cry not only from legalism but also from pure law-ethics. It has ample room to accommodate concerns both of act-morality and agent-morality or what nowadays is dubbed "virtue-ethics."[11] Similarly, Jewish Covenantal Ethics is both self-regarding and other-regarding. Because of its pluralistic thrust, it can readily distinguish between the demands of public and private morality. There is no *a priori* requirement that the same set of moral norms guide both domains. As we shall see later, in the discussion on the ethics of warfare, it makes perfect sense to maintain that a state may legitimately act in a manner that would be totally improper for individuals. To be sure, that does not amount to an endorsement of Reinhold Niebuhr's advocacy of "Moral Realism" and the rejection of moral absolutes. From the perspective of Jewish Covenantal Ethics, states, too, are bound by moral absolutes. But the absolute moral principles governing the policies of a state need not necessarily coincide with those applicable to the conduct of individuals.[12]

In view of the crucial role played by intuition in the complex art of ethical decision-making, it is important to consider the factors that influence the formation of an individual's ethical perceptions. There can be no doubt that the ethos of a given society plays a large role in the development of the human conscience (or the superego). Insofar as Jewish Covenantal Ethics is concerned, a variety of sources can qualify as legitimate and proper matrices of Jewish ethical intuitions. To begin with, as I indicated previously in the discussion of Nachmanides' views, the study of the specific laws of the Covenant enables us to grasp the meaning of the broad ethical principles contained in the Torah. In addition, moral conduct in conformity with the specific norms of the Torah exerts a profound influence upon the formation of our attitudes. One need not adopt the James-Lange theory of emotions in order to appreciate the significance of behavior patterns on the development of ethical dispositions.[13] The Rabbinic Sages already declared that "the commandments were given for the purpose of ennobling human beings."[14] I elaborate upon this later, in the discussion of agent-morality.

There are also numerous nonlegal aspects of Judaism that influence the formation of ethical responses characterizing a Covenantal ethos. In his Preface to his Commentary on the Babylonian Talmud, Rabbi Moses Edeles called attention to the role played by the Aggadah as a source of guidance on matters pertaining to *Mussar* (ethico-religious attitudes). Rabbi Tzvi Yehudah Berlin maintains that the reason the Torah does not merely contain laws but also devotes almost the entire book of Genesis to relate historic material about the Patriarchs is to provide us with religious and ethical models for guiding our ethical judgments.[15] In his view, the various moral laws of the Torah by themselves would not have been adequate to this task.

Rabbi Soloveitchik also maintains that ethics cannot be reduced to formal rules. Cultivation of intuitive faculties is needed for formation of proper ethical judgments. In his opinion, various encomia of God are included in the liturgy for the purpose of exposing the worshiper to the various moral ideals that make up *imitatio Dei*.[16] God is beyond all praise and obviously does not need it. But we celebrate and extol His moral attributes in order to give direction to the worshiper in the never-ending quest for ethical perfection.

One of the most basic requirements for the cultivation of moral sensitivity, according to Rabbi Soloveitchik, is the availability of appropriate role models. That is why, in his opinion, the Talmud declares that personal contact with scholars is more important than the mastery of their formal opinions.[17]

The thesis that following the personal example set by outstanding ethical personalities is vitally necessary for cultivating a proper ethical outlook is by no means original to Rabbi Soloveitchik, but represents one of the salient features of the Maimonidean system. Significantly, Maimonides includes the commandment, "Thou shalt cleave to Him," which he interprets as the obligation to attach oneself to scholars qualified to function as models for ethico-religious conduct, in the section of the *Code* setting forth his views on morality rather than, as might be expected, in the section dealing with *Talmud Torah* (the study of the Torah).[18] Maimonides placed this commandment in *Hilkhot Deot* because he adopted the Aristotelian premise that virtue can only be defined ostensively—that is, in terms of the virtuous conduct of individuals renowned for practical wisdom. Thus, he did not attempt to delineate the exact nature of the various desirable traits of character but maintained that they can only be communicated by the example set by eminent scholars of the Law whose conduct is worthy of emulation.[19]

Because the intuitions of Covenantal Ethics are engendered by a multiplicity of sources that frequently stress divergent values, it should hardly be surprising that the Jewish tradition contains such a variety of mutually exclusive ethical ideals, ranging from the advocacy of asceticism as a supreme religious goal to the endorsement of indulgence in legitimate pleasures, from advocating participation in worldly affairs to counseling maximum withdrawal from the secular sphere. To be sure, disagreements on substantive issues are by no means limited to the nonlegal components of Judaism; they affect Halakhah as well. But there remains one important difference. Halakhah contains provisions (for example, majority rule) for the resolution of conflicting opinions in the realm of practice. But no such procedure is available for nonlegal issues. Theoretical truth cannot be determined by majority vote. Moreover, even in matters of conduct there is no guarantee that the majority is right. The majority can confer only legitimacy, but not truth or correctness, upon a given legal opinion. Moral propriety, as opposed to legality, cannot be based on processes patterned after legal institutions.

In areas where halakhic guidance is unavailable there is no mechanism by which competing moral claims can be adjudicated. Individuals who seek to go beyond mere legal requirements, in their quest for an all-encompassing life of piety, have no alternative but to rely either on their own personal moral perceptions or seek guidance from other individuals who are regarded by them as moral authorities. The latter, in turn, must rely on their equally subjective intuitions.

CHAPTER THREE

General Welfare & Morality

IT IS GENERALLY AGREED THAT CONSIDERATIONS of social utility play a dominant role in the formation of ethical beliefs. Utilitarians define goodness in terms of social utility. But even many philosophers (for example, Plato, Aristotle, and Hume) who are not prepared to *define* goodness in terms of utility nonetheless recognize that our moral beliefs reflect concern for the general welfare. Even Kant, who in his rigorous formalism insisted that the ethical propriety of an act depends solely upon the universalizability of its motive and has nothing to do with the ensuing consequences, made room for utilitarian concerns when he formulated his conception of "imperfect duties."

I

Although Jewish Covenantal Ethics is based upon a variety of independent norms that need not be deducible from any single principle, the promotion of social harmony and peace plays a pivotal role. Maimonides goes so far as to declare that the promotion of peace is the very objective of the Torah's moral legislation.[1] There is, of course, ample talmudic precedent for this view. Basing itself upon the biblical verse, "[I]ts ways are the ways of pleasantness and all its paths are peaceful" (Proverbs

3:17), the Talmud maintains that the entire Torah is designed to promote *darkhei shalom* (the ways of peace).[2] The Rabbis derived from this verse the technical term "the ways of peace," which they invoked both as a hermeneutical rule for the analysis of ambiguous texts[3] and as the ground for many of their own enactments.[4] Indeed, the active pursuit of peace is extolled as one of the foremost religious obligations.[5] Moreover, the midrashic literature frequently points out that without peace, all other blessings become worthless.[6] The tradition extols ideal religious personalities, the *talmidei chakhamim* (the scholars of the Law), for increasing the peace of the world.[7] Some halakhic authorities even contended that the word *shalom* (peace) must be revered as a "name of God."[8] In the striking formulation of the Zohar, "He who opposes peace, opposes the Holy Name."[9] The Torah even permitted the erasure of the name of God if necessary for the preservation of *shalom bayit* (domestic peace),[10] as in the case of a *sotah* (a wife suspected of infidelity).

Because peace plays such a pre-eminent role among Jewish moral values, it is not surprising that the pursuit of peace takes precedence over many other ethical obligations. Notwithstanding the fact that the Sages extol truth as "the seal of the Holy One, blessed be He,"[11] they grant that one may, in the interest of preserving or restoring peace, not only conceal the truth but actually deviate from it and tell an outright lie.[12] Medieval authorities, however, disagree as to whether a concern for peace is the only justification for concealing the truth or whether there are additional, *independent* considerations that warrant setting aside the requirement of truthfulness. Rashi operates with a relatively narrow definition of peace and maintains that the requirements of modesty, humility, or sensitivity are independent justifications for concealing the truth.[13] The Tosaphists, on the other hand, subsume the various cases where the Talmud explicitly sanctions deviating from the truth under a liberally interpreted definition of the "ways of peace."

So pronounced is the emphasis upon peace both in biblical and rabbinic literature that in his pioneering work, *The Ethics of Judaism,* Moritz Lazarus cites the talmudic statement that "the

entire Torah seeks to promote the ways of peace"[14] to support
the thesis that the sole purpose of the Torah is to advance peace
and harmony within society.[15] Of course, this talmudic passage
in itself can hardly be construed as evidence for his pan-ethical
approach to Judaism, which, in the spirit of Kant, would regard
religion as a handmaiden of ethics and reduce the entire scope
and function of religion to a mere means of promoting ethical
values. The passage only shows that the observance of the Torah
is conducive to the harmonious functioning of society. This is a
far cry from holding that the creation of a peaceful society represents the be-all and end-all of the entire Torah.

Numerous sources buttress the view that Jewish ethical principles are based upon concern for the well-being of society. The
Bible frequently concludes its appeals for compliance with the
provisions of the Covenant by stating that such provisions are
intended for our own good.[16] Maimonides unequivocally declares that the ethical laws of the Torah are designed for the improvement of the material well-being of society:

> As for the well-being of the body, it comes about by the improve-
> ment of their ways of living one with another. This is achieved
> through two things. One of them is the abolition of their wronging
> each other. This is tantamount to every individual among the people
> not being permitted to act according to his will and up to the limits
> of his power, but being forced to do that which is useful to the
> whole. The second thing consists in the acquisition by every human
> individual of moral qualities that are useful for life in society so that
> the affairs of the city may be ordered.[17]

Since ethical conduct is conducive to the common good,
obeying the Torah's moral legislation confers this-worldly benefits upon society as a whole. Moreover, Maimonides takes it for
granted that individuals performing moral acts are bound to
benefit from the improved social conditions engendered by their
behavior. This, in Maimonides' opinion, accounts for the traditional distinction that is made between the rewards that are received for the fulfillment of moral versus ritual commandments.
Whereas observance of the commandments between human be-

ings and God yields only spiritual rewards in the world-to-come, commandments governing relations between people belong to a different category. While their spiritual reward, too, is reaped only in the hereafter, there are this-worldly benefits as well:

> When man fulfills the commandments which are based upon utility for human beings . . . he will obtain good in this world. His having engaged in a good practice will influence others to do likewise and he will in turn benefit from this practice.[18]

This emphasis upon the social benefits of moral laws also has important legal ramifications. Although as a general rule, according to Maimonides, the death penalty can be imposed only when the perpetrator of a capital crime has been properly warned by two witnesses prior to committing the crime, we make an exception in the case of a murderer. The reason we are stricter with a person who killed an individual than with one guilty of idolatry, an even more serious offense, is that the murderer commits a crime that imperils the very survival of society. Maimonides cites the verse, "A man that is laden with the blood of any person shall hasten his steps into the pit; none shall support him" (Proverbs 28:17) as prooftext that killing is such a horrendous crime that it outweighs all the good a person has accomplished.[19]

In stressing the close connection between morality and social utility, Maimonides hardly broke any new ground, but followed in the footsteps of many of his predecessors. In the tenth century, Saadiah Gaon classified ethical commandments as rational, not merely revelational, because he attributed to them a socially beneficial purpose. Judah Halevi, too, harped upon the utility of the ethical commandments and insisted that no society could survive without morality. Even a gang of robbers, he states, cannot function without a set of rules of conduct. But in his opinion, it is impossible to establish a lasting moral consensus solely on a rational basis. For this reason, most societies contain within themselves the seeds of their own destruction. They are ultimately bound to disintegrate, because no man-made moral sys-

tem is capable of resisting erosion by inevitable historical transformations. The Jewish moral system, on the other hand, rests
on divinely revealed laws, which are impervious to the vicissi-
tudes of historical change. Hence, while all other nations sooner
or later disappear, the Jewish nation alone is eternal.[20]

Nachmanides also takes the social utility of moral laws for
granted. In a striking comment he points out that Jewish survival and social stability in the Land of Israel hinge primarily
upon the observance of the *mishpatim* — that is, ethical laws —
rather than obedience to the entire Torah.[21] The belief that the
viability of society depends upon morality is clearly expressed in
R. Jacob Ben Asher's *Tur Choshen Mishpat,* a classic code of Jewish law. Noting the apparent contradiction between the statement attributed to Rabban Shimon Ben Gamliel in *Pirkei Avot,*
that "the world endures by virtue of truth, law and peace,"[22] and
that of Shimon the Just, who maintained that "the world is
based upon Torah, service and benevolent actions,"[23] the author
of the *Tur* suggests a rather plausible explanation.[24] Whereas the
former statement addresses itself to the question of why the universe exists, the latter deals with the necessary *conditions* for its
survival. In other words, ethical values are indispensable to the
proper functioning of human society.

This stance closely resembles the position of Judah Halevi.
He argued that although the prophets, while seeming to disregard transgressions of ritual laws, harped so much upon violations of the ethical laws, this does not mean that they deemed
the latter religiously superior. On the contrary, in Halevi's
scheme, ritual laws play a far more significant role than ethical
precepts in the development of the *inyan ha-E-lohi,* the religious
faculty that, in his opinion, is exclusively granted to Jews. What
troubled the prophets, according to the *Sefer ha-Kuzari,* was the
fact that the Jewish people had degenerated to such an extent
that they flouted even the ethical laws, without which no human
society can survive.[25]

Interestingly, Bahya Ben Asher Ben Chlava, in his homiletical
treatise *Kad Ha-kemach,* cites the very rationality of the ethical
laws and their social indispensability as the reason we do not

recite a *berakhah* (a blessing) prior to performing acts of lovingkindness such as dispensing charitable gifts or visiting the sick, whereas we do recite a blessing before carrying out a ritual obligation such as donning tefillin or hearing the shofar. Since the blessings recited prior to the performance of a mitzvah contain the expression, "He who has sanctified us through His commandments and commanded us to . . . ," it would be inappropriate in his opinion to say these words when the performance of the action is mandated by the promptings of the human conscience rather than by the Revelation vouchsafed to Israel alone.[26]

Joseph Albo also recognizes the link between morality and utility. He takes it for granted that ethical norms are based upon natural or conventional laws, which are deemed conducive to the collective well-being of society.[27]

Closely akin to this conception is the position of a recent, widely quoted Rabbinic scholar, Rabbi Meir Simchah of Dvinsk. He notes that while from the perspective of personal piety, acts of theft, robbery, and violence do not represent as serious violations of the Torah as do idolatry and sexual corruption, their impact upon society is far more devastating than that of other sins. While society as a whole can survive idolatry and other major breaches of the Torah, it is bound to disintegrate whenever basic ethical norms are violated. Thus, he explains why, according to Rabbinic interpretation, the flood was inflicted as punishment for the sin of violence rather than for other more grievous offenses that were committed.[28]

In the opinion of R. Akiva,[29] the Jewish ethical code is founded upon the principle "Love thy neighbor as thyself." It is not content with enjoining malfeasance but mandates beneficence. Malicious selfishness — for example, denying another person the use of one's possessions, at no cost to oneself — is denounced as *midat Sedom*,[30] conduct characteristic of Sodom. While in modern Western usage "sodomy" describes sexual offenses, the Jewish tradition employs the term *midat Sedom* to denote unmitigated selfishness and utter indifference to the well-being of others. In keeping with the centrality of altruism in Jewish ethics, the Mishnah states, "He who declares, 'mine is mine, and yours is yours,' displays the characteristics of Sodom."[31] The Tannaitic opinion, that Sodom's moral depravity manifested itself primarily in unmitigated selfishness rather than in sexual perversion, echoes the words of the prophet Ezekiel:

> Behold, this was the iniquity of thy sister Sodom: Pride, fulness of bread, and careless ease was in her and her daughters, neither did she strengthen the hand of the poor and the needy.[32]

Rabbinic law regards concern for the welfare of others as so obligatory that it even becomes a factor in considerations of equity.[33] Many provisions of the Torah can be invoked as precedents for this approach. For example, the Torah does not merely prohibit depriving other individuals of their possessions but mandates that even if we merely spot someone else's lost possession, we must attempt to recover it and return it to the owner.[34] According to Rabbinic interpretation, this commandment includes the duty to protect an individual against the loss of life or limb. Maimonides cites this law as the source of a physician's obligation to treat patients.[35] Similarly, the verse "thou shalt not stand by the blood of your brother" is interpreted in talmudic literature as an obligation to act as a "good Samaritan" and assist others when their lives are endangered.[36]

Altruism is not merely a religious duty but at times creates outright legally enforceable obligations. So strong is the condemnation of selfishness that, in situations characterized by the Talmud as falling under the category of "this one benefits, and the other one does not lose anything," a court may coerce an owner to let someone else use vacant property, since there is no cost to the proprietor.[37]

The Torah even imposes an outright obligation to expend one's property to help the destitute. To deliberately disregard this obligation to help others is to deny all that Judaism represents. As R. Joshua ben Korcha put it, "He who closes his eyes against charity is like an idolator."[38] The Amora Ulla declared that it is only through the practice of *tzedakah* that the Redemption will be achieved.[39] It has often been pointed out that the Hebrew term for charity, *tzedakah,* is derived from the root *tzedek* (righteousness). Thus, the giving of charity stems from the requirement that we do justice.

Although our needy fellow human beings are not entitled to take our possessions, they have a legitimate claim to our assistance. We are obligated to help them because we owe them our love. As Paul Tillich suggests, justice is not the antithesis of love but rather calls for the proper distribution of love.[40]

Concern for the well-being of others must not be limited to solicitude for their material welfare. According to Rabbinic interpretation, the phrase "Thou shalt rebuke thy neighbor" (Leviticus 19:17), which precedes the biblical formulation of the love imperative, mandates not only that we bring to the attention of our fellow human beings what we perceive to be wrongs they have done to us, in order to forestall our bearing grudges or harboring resentment against them, but also calls for solicitude for their spiritual welfare and imposes upon us the obligation to attempt to influence them to abide by the norms of the Torah.[41]

II

Rabbinic legislation reflects extraordinary sensitivity to the requirements both of altruism and societal harmony. A large number of ordinances have been enacted for the sake of *tikkun ha-olam* (the improvement of the world).[42] Moreover, concern for "the ways of peace," or the prevention of *eivah* (animosity), inspired a considerable number of Rabbinic decrees supplementing and at times even modifying biblical laws on the ground that "its [the Torah's] ways are the ways of pleasantness and all its paths are peace."[43] In the words of the Mishnah,

> These things were said on account of the ways of peace: A Cohen reads the Torah first, then a Levi, and after him a regular Israelite. An *Eruv* must be deposited in an old house [its usual place] on account of the ways of peace. . . . If one takes possession of trapped animals, birds and fish, it is considered robbery on account of the ways of peace. . . . If one takes possession of what was found by a

deaf-mute, an insane person, or a minor, it is considered robbery on account of the ways of peace. . . . One does not restrain poor pagans from collecting the gleanings, forgotten pieces and what is left on the corners of fields on account of the ways of peace.[44]

This last provision is expanded in the Talmud on the basis of a *baraita,* which states:

One supports poor non-Jews together with poor Israelites, and one visits sick non-Jews together with sick Israelites, and one buries dead non-Jews as one buries dead Israelites on account of the ways of peace.[45]

There is considerable disagreement in the post-talmudic literature about the purpose of the Rabbinic decree that we are obligated to help non-Jews, despite the fact that, according to the Torah, we are commanded to support only needy members of the Covenantal community. Are these and similar measures designed to generate goodwill among non-Jews and therefore intended to serve the self-interest of the Jewish community? Or are we dealing here with a genuine moral concern that transcends purely pragmatic or prudential considerations? There are no easy answers to this question. It appears that many differences of opinion among Jewish legal authorities can be traced back to different conceptual approaches to the meaning of "the ways of peace."

An array of prominent Jewish scholars such as Professors Hoffmann,[46] Lazarus,[47] and Lauterbach[48] regard "the ways of peace" as an intrinsic moral value and categorically reject any suggestion that the concern for the "the ways of peace" revolves around pragmatic considerations of Jewish self-interest. But it appears that their views were not so much based upon an objective evaluation of the sources as inspired by apologetic fervor. Their primary aim was to counteract Christian polemicists, who, in their eagerness to demonstrate the alleged superiority of Christian universalism over Jewish particularism, claimed that the "ways of peace" amounted merely to a prudential device to ensure co-existence with the non-Jewish world. In what strikes us an an overreaction to tendentious Christian "scholarship," they went to the other extreme and rejected any suggestion that the traditional Jewish concern for "the ways of peace" had any connection with purely pragmatic considerations of Jewish self-interest and expediency. Supplementing the previously cited argument that the entire Torah was exclusively designed as an instrument to promote harmony and peace,[49] they seek to fortify their case by reading into the term "the ways of peace" their own preconceived notions. Thus, they argue that if the expression "the ways of peace" were merely intended to designate prevention of animosity between individuals, more narrowly focused terms such as *devar ha-shalom* (in the interest of peace) or *mipnei eivah* (prevention of animosity) rather than the more wide-ranging *darkhei shalom,* would have been much more appropriate. That the Rabbis employed the more inclusive term, "the ways of peace," supposedly proves that their ordinances were enacted as measures designed to achieve not merely the relatively limited goal of social stability but also to advance the sublime ethical ideal of *shalom,* in the broadest sense of the term.

This argument, however, collapses once we note that the Talmud uses the positive formulation *mipnei darkhei shalom* and the negative formulation *mipnei eivah* interchangeably. As a matter of fact, many ordinances for which Tannaitic sources give no reasons but which resemble the kind of enactments that the Mishnah justified on the ground of *darkhei shalom* are explained in the Gemara as necessary for the prevention of *eivah.* Thus, there is no conceptual difference between the two formulations, which, for all practical purposes, are equivalent.[50] It thus appears that what in earlier periods was termed *darkhei shalom* became, as the result of a later change in terminology, *mipnei eivah.*

One might, of course, contend that even if the enactments that fall under the rubric of *darkhei shalom* amounted merely to measures designed to keep the peace and prevent friction, they still could be endowed with enormous moral significance, since Judaism is closer to Aristotle than to Kant and refuses to make absolute distinctions between prudence and morality. But we are still left with the question of whether charitable acts performed

ETHICS OF RESPONSIBILITY

in the interest of peace represent intrinsic or instrumental ethical values.

Upon closer examination, it becomes evident that neither the one-sided views expressed by the previously cited Jewish scholars nor those of their Christian counterparts are completely accurate. As a matter of fact, support for both positions can be marshalled from traditional sources. Some medieval halakhic authorities operated within a narrow ethnocentric framework, restricting the applicability of regulations based upon "the ways of peace" or "the prevention of animosity" to periods when Jews depended upon the goodwill of the non-Jewish world. Moreover, some highly respected legists claimed that even during periods when Jews must be concerned with the reaction of the non-Jewish world, they should merely avoid giving offense through overt discrimination against non-Jews in the distribution of charity. But, they argue that, as long as failure to assist non-Jews would not be perceived as a discriminatory act, there is no obligation to extend oneself in behalf of non-Jews.[51]

Maimonides, however, disagrees with this position and makes it abundantly clear that the notion "the ways of peace" reflects not merely pragmatic considerations of Jewish self-interest but expresses sublime ethico-religious ideals.[52] Especially telling is his formulation in the concluding paragraph of chapter 10 of his "Laws of Kings":

> The Sages commanded us to to visit the sick of the pagans and to bury their dead together with the dead of the Israelites and to support their poor amidst the poor of the Israelites to promote the ways of peace. As it is said: "God is good to all and His compassion extends to all His creatures" [Psalms 145:9]. And it is said: "Its ways are the ways of pleasantness and all its paths are peace."[53]

In this peroration, Maimonides quotes as prooftext for "the ways of peace" a biblical source that is not mentioned in the Talmud. Why did Maimonides find it necessary to adduce an additional scriptural source, instead of relying exclusively on the biblical passage, "Its ways . . . are peace," which, according to the Talmud, serves as the *sole* biblical basis of "the ways of peace"?

To answer this question, we refer to Maimonides' statement at the conclusion of "The Laws of Slaves":

> With respect to the moral attributes of God that we are commanded to imitate, it is said "and His mercy extends to all."[54]

Maimonides, apparently, seeks to guard against the misconception that the various laws mandating philanthropy to non-Jews are merely devised to serve Jewish self-interest. He, therefore, cites a biblical verse making it clear that the prescribed practices represent vital components of the religious imperative to engage in *imitatio Dei*.[55]

By linking the pursuit of "the ways of peace" with the emulation of the divine attribute of compassion, Maimonides suggests that even in situations in which, for technical reasons, certain provisions of act-morality may be inapplicable, considerations of agent-morality form the matrix of additional obligations. Although the Torah's commandment prescribing alms-giving does not include an obligation to support non-Jewish poor people, agent-morality dictates that we display compassion to all individuals regardless of their ethnic or religious background. Whereas Jewish act-morality contains features that differentiate between members and non-members of the Covenantal community, agent-morality makes no distinctions. Insensitivity to the needs of others is no less reprehensible when it is displayed in one's conduct toward non-Jews than it would be toward Jews. A more extensive discussion of agent-morality is reserved for chapter 5 of this book.

To return to the specific issue of the ways of peace vis-à-vis non-Jews, the *Code* contains a passage that at first blush seems to suggest that Maimonides, too, subscribes to the thesis that the various ordinances enacted out of concern for "the ways of peace" merely serve the purposes of Jewish self-interest. Writing in the "Laws of Idolatry," after mentioning a variety of practices mandated or legitimated by considerations of *darkhei shalom*, he adds the following qualification:

> These rules apply only when Israel is exiled among the Gentiles or when the Gentiles are in a position of superior strength. But when

Jews are in a position of superior strength, we are not permitted to suffer *idol-worshiping* Gentiles among us [emphasis added].[56]

This passage, however, does not really conflict with the Maimonidean thesis that the practice of philanthropy toward non-Jews is a *religious* obligation.[57] The fact that, under certain conditions, ordinances pertaining to *darkhei shalom* are inapplicable within the borders of the Land of Israel does not at all indicate that they are viewed as mere counsels of expediency devoid of intrinsic moral significance. What prompts Maimonides to make a statement that strikes the modern mind as a manifestation of extreme intolerance and xenophobia is his deep-rooted abhorrence of idolatry, which gives rise to his extremely stringent view that idolators are prohibited even from entering, let alone residing in, the Land of Israel, lest exposure to their beliefs and practices corrode the faith of the believers in God.[58] But this by no means detracts from the religious significance attached to the practice of "the ways of peace" toward Jews and non-Jews alike. It is simply the case that, for Maimonides, the fear of the possible spread of idolatry is such an overriding consideration that even concern for "the ways of peace" must be subordinated to it.

CHAPTER FOUR

Pleasure & Goodness

I N THE LAST CHAPTER WE FOCUSED UPON THE SO-
cial utility of morality. We now examine the scope and limitations of concern for the general welfare. We also discuss
additional factors that must be considered in Jewish ethics.

I

We have seen that, in the opinion of Maimonides and many
other authorities, moral norms are based upon considerations
involving the material well-being of society. This explanation reflects the positive attitude of the Jewish tradition toward enjoyment of material satisfactions. As opposed to Puritanism, pleasures are treated as intrinsic goods. Conversely, suffering and
pain are regarded as evils to be avoided. In a daring metaphor,
the Rabbis assert that God Himself suffers whenever human beings are in anguish.[1]

The high valuation of human pleasure and the concomitant
aversion to pain, however, do not prevent the Rabbis from
maintaining that adversity has a positive side as well. Want and
misery, by inspiring human efforts to combat them, prod human beings to fulfill their task of becoming partners with God
in completing the process of Creation. Moreover, the experience
of pain or misery may also be conducive to attaining a variety of

spiritual goods. We frequently develop our capacity for empathy, compassion, and humility as the result of suffering. Moreover, the Rabbis extoll the role of suffering in the expiation of sins and the process of atonement. Suffering is credited with helping human beings attain the bliss of the hereafter.[2] Hardship, deprivation, and pain frequently engender a sense of dependence upon God and lead to spiritual regeneration. Since the experience of suffering may result in a spiritual boon, it may even be welcomed at times as a manifestation of divine love. In the words of Proverbs (3:12), "For whom God loveth, He chastiseth." In this spirit, the Tannaim developed the doctrine of *yissurin shel ahavah* (suffering due to love).[3]

But it is one thing to declare that some good may be extracted from suffering and another to treat suffering as desirable. In itself, suffering is an evil. But the tradition teaches us that evil was, nevertheless, created by an omnibenevolent God, because its existence was necessary in order for the world to contain the greatest possible amount of good. An ancient Midrash informs us that it was only on account of the presence of evil and suffering in the universe that God pronounced His Creation not merely as good but as *very good*.[4] In other words, the existence of suffering is a necessary condition for a world of maximum goodness, since in its absence many values and goods could not have come into being.

Both Jewish and non-Jewish religious writings abound with attempts at theodicies, purporting to show why various particular evils were necessary for the world to contain maximum goodness.[5] In the wake of the Holocaust, theologians were challenged to explain how such horrendous tragedies could be reconciled with belief in an omnipotent and benevolent God.[6] Discussion of this issue is beyond the limited scope of this book. Suffice it to state that it makes perfect sense to argue that from a divine perspective all evil must be necessary, even if, from our limited understanding, we cannot fathom the reason for its necessity. Rabbi Soloveitchik has argued that instead of engaging in a futile search for metaphysical explanations of evil, we should respond to suffering as a challenge to convert it into a source of some good that otherwise would not have been obtained.[7]

The belief that suffering may be necessary to realize the greatest possible good by no means justifies apathy to *avoidable* suffering. We must not lose sight of the fact that, however beneficial the ensuing consequences, intrinsically, any form of suffering is an evil. For example, sickness may arouse us from our spiritual slumbers and induce contrition, repentance, and spiritual regeneration. We are, nonetheless, mandated to heal the sick and alleviate their pain.[8] As a matter of fact, Jewish law waives many requirements and lifts many restrictions in situations where compliance with Rabbinic ordinances would cause considerable pain or excessive discomfort.[9]

Because of its aversion to unnecessary suffering, the Jewish tradition frowns upon excessive self-denial and self-mortification. Asceticism has been encouraged only to the extent that it serves as a means to attain higher spiritual values. Representative of the highly ambivalent attitude displayed toward asceticism as a spiritual discipline are the sharp differences of opinion as to whether Nazarites who voluntarily deprive themselves of legitimate pleasures should be regarded as saints or sinners.[10] But it is apparent that even those who recommend asceticism as a religious ideal do so only because they deem it useful as a means to attain piety, not because they grant suffering the status of an intrinsic value or of an end in itself.

Similarly, unlike some other religions, Judaism does not look upon poverty as a badge of merit but as a challenge to overcome it. The solicitude that the Torah and the rest of Scriptures express for the weak, the poor, and the disadvantaged reflects not their superior status but rather God's profound concern for their suffering. Since God cares so much for their plight, human beings have a special responsibility to ameliorate it.

Despite the fact that the Bible and Rabbinic literature time and again warn against the hazards of affluence and extol the spiritual benefits that may accrue from poverty,[11] we are obligated to help the indigent and, for that matter, to refrain from practices that result in our own pauperization.[12] In the words of Maimonides:

> A person should never give all his property to the sanctuary. He who engages in this practice transgresses the intent of Scripture. . . . This is not piety but folly because he loses all property and he will have to depend upon others. . . . It is with regard to him and similar other cases that the Rabbis stated that pious fools destroy the world.[13]

Judaism looks upon wealth and power as blessings that must be handled with care lest they wreak havoc with our spiritual well-being. But it does not subscribe to the Calvinistic doctrine that material success is an index of spiritual worth. Equally unacceptable is the Lutheran conception that as stewards of God's blessings, human beings have a religious obligation to augment them as much as possible. On the contrary, excessive preoccupation with material success is regarded as a serious impediment to the study of Torah, which, in the Jewish hierarchy of values, ranks above contributions to the enhancement of the material welfare of society. "To make possible the concentration upon the study of the Torah, the ideal religious personality . . . is urged to forego, if necessary, the satisfaction of many legitimate needs."[14]

The recommendation to suffer deprivation for the sake of spiritual gains, however, does not indicate a negative attitude toward material well-being as such. It is simply a case of sacrificing a lower value for the sake of a higher value, for spiritual satisfactions rank higher than material satisfactions. Far from being a spiritual handicap, material well-being may even be a boon to spiritual growth. This becomes evident from the fact, according to a talmudic opinion, that affluence is a necessary qualification for prophecy.[15]

Notwithstanding the Midrash's assertion that the spiritual gains of the donor outweigh the benefits derived by the recipient,[16] the main goal of charity is not the improvement of the spiritual well-being of the donor, but the reduction of the suffering of the recipient.[17] This approach differs from that of some Christian sects. Because of their other-worldly orientation, they are basically indifferent to deprivation or want. To them, alms-giving primarily is a religious exercise yielding spiritual benefits to the donor—not an activity designed to alleviate the plight of the needy.[18]

Our preceding discussion clearly shows that nothing is further from the Jewish ethos than the notion that the prevalence of misery and pain indicates that it is willed by God and that, therefore, any human intervention to alleviate suffering contravenes the Divine Providential design. The Talmud reports a dialogue on the subject between the Roman general Turnus Rufus and the Jewish sage Rabbi Akiva. The Roman general challenged Akiva: If God loves the poor, why does He not support them? Akiva replied: God permits suffering in the world in order to provide man with a sense of mission—to imitate the Creator through the performance of acts of *chesed* (lovingkindness.) A gift to the poor, therefore, far from subverting God's purposes, is a gift to God,[19] Who has entrusted man with the task of completing the process of Creation by eliminating as much as possible all avoidable suffering.

II

Yet, for all its emphasis upon human welfare and the need to maximize pleasure and minimize pain, Judaism by no means defines good and evil in a purely hedonistic or utilitarian fashion. Pleasure (whether for egotistical hedonism of the agent, or for utilitarianism, the total aggregate of pleasure experienced by society) cannot be the sole criterion. Judaism is a mitzvah-centered rather than a salvation-centered religion. The purpose of life is not simply to attain supreme bliss, but to realize God's purpose for man. Thus, though the Tanna R. Yaacov looked upon this world merely as "a vestibule to the world-to-come"[20] and maintained that "one hour of satisfaction in the world-to-come outweighs all the satisfactions of this world,"[21] he nonetheless contended that "one hour spent in repentance and the performance of good deeds outweighs all of the life of the world-to-come."[22] Since the human task can be carried out only in our transient spatio-temporal world but not in the higher regions where we may receive our ultimate reward, the Jewish value system attaches enormous significance to life in the here-and-now, which is the exclusive arena for the fulfillment of the norms of the Torah.[23]

Judaism recognizes the pragmatic value of appeals to self-interest as prods to ethical conduct. Thus, Maimonides concludes the first chapter of his ethical treatise with the peroration that "he who walks in this way [the way of God] brings good and blessing upon himself."[24] He also recommends that in rebuking a sinner, one should remind him that "he sins against himself by his evil actions."[25] Moreover, one should make clear to the offender that one "talks to him only for his own good to bring him to the life of the world-to-come."[26] But as one rises to higher levels of religious piety, obedience to God's will, in sharp contrast with Aquinas's approach, should not be motivated by the desire to enjoy the bliss associated with our ultimate return to the source of our being. Ideally, one should banish all self-regarding motives. For Maimonides, the real reward for the performance of a mitzvah is that it will engender the performance of another mitzvah.[27] It is only when one has succeeded in completely overcoming all interest in personal gratification from the performance of a mitzvah that one can be described as "one who serves God out of pure love."[28]

Some classical Jewish thinkers do not share Maimonides' opinion that aiming for the purely spiritual benefits in the hereafter should fall under the category of ulterior motives that detract from the religious value of good deeds. Saadiah Gaon, for example, contends that Abraham was willing to offer his son as a sacrifice only because worldly satisfactions paled into insignificance compared with the bliss of the hereafter.[29] Even more emphasis is placed upon spiritual rewards by Isaac Arama. He not only refuses to relegate those seeking reward in the hereafter to a lower level of piety, but insists that expecting spiritual reward from the fulfillment of a divine commandment is an essential feature of performing a mitzvah.[30] But even these thinkers admit that, while the expectation of reward is a perfectly legitimate motive for religious conduct, it must not become the exclusive motive. Obviously, they would not challenge the authority of the Mishnah, which declared:

> Antigonus of Sokho said: "Be not like servants who serve their master in order to receive reward."[31]

Similarly, another Tannaitic source warns against self-seeking motivations in the performance of religious commandments:

> You might perhaps say, "I want to study Torah so that I may be called a scholar, so that I may be able to join the Academy, or that I may enjoy a long life in the world-to-come," therefore the Torah states "to love [God]," study at any rate and the glory will eventually arrive.[32]

III

There are, however, even more compelling reasons for rejecting the hedonistic doctrine that ethics revolves exclusively around considerations of pleasure or pain. As the bearer of the image of God, each human being possesses irreducible dignity, sanctity, and inviolability. Quantitative or qualitative factors do not affect that status. According to the Tanna Ben Azzai, this is the pivotal doctrine of the entire Torah.[33]

Concern for the sanctity of life always overrides considerations of social utility. It is categorically prohibited to commit suicide or to kill an innocent person, no matter how much such acts would contribute to the general welfare. "Active euthanasia," however noble the motive, can never be condoned, even if intended solely for the purpose of ending the suffering of a patient.

Because of the absolute sanctity of every human life, it is strictly forbidden to take one life in order to save another life, however valuable.[34] One may not sacrifice even one individual in order to save a large number of people.[35] The only exception to this rule is when dealing with an aggressor. Be it in self-defense or in defense of another person, if there is no other way to save the victim, Jewish law mandates that one should kill the aggressor.

Similar considerations rule out accepting the offer of terminally ill persons to sacrifice their lives for the benefit of another individual. However hopeless their condition, they are not permitted to donate their organs for transplants, if the procedures will inevitably shorten their lives — even if only by a few minutes.[36] Depriving an individual of *chayei sha'ah* (a minimal duration of life) represents an act of killing, which cannot be condoned.[37] Obviously, were our ethical norms solely based upon social utility, we would adopt an entirely different attitude. But since the overriding concern for the sanctity of life is based upon the biblical doctrine that "God created man in His image,"[38] it is totally irrelevant that the donor of the organ is anyhow on the verge of death, whereas the prospective recipient might yet make vital contributions to society. As bearers of the image of God, both possess equal value.

But in the biblical ethos, only human individuals possess infinite value. In the account of the creation of plants, reptiles, or mammals, the Bible notes that they were created "according to their species." Significantly, there is no reference to the species in the biblical story depicting the creation of humanity. As the Mishnah declares, "Adam was created as a single individual . . . therefore, one who destroys a single human life is regarded as having destroyed the entire universe."[39] Bearing the divine image, human beings transcend the realm of nature and enjoy a special status among creatures.[40]

Although the Bible mandates compassion for all creatures, Judaism balks at the extreme formulations of reverence for all life that undergird the agenda of the animal rights movement. The Jewish value-system insists that there is a radical difference between humans and animals. Only human beings are so sacred that they must not be sacrificed even for the collective good. Treatment of animals, on the other hand, is not subject to the overriding constraints of inviolable rights,[41] but should be governed by utilitarian considerations.

Unlike the advocates of animal rights, who are so wary of inflicting pain upon animals that they even object to their use for medical research, Halakhah sanctions whatever experiments on animals are necessary to help humans in the battle against disease. From a Jewish perspective, the imperative mandating the preservation of human life and the alleviation of suffering overrides the prohibition against torturing animals. However, all possible measures must be taken to minimize the pain of animals, since cruelty to animals is strictly prohibited.

Experimentation on human beings, on the other hand, is subject to completely different standards. The inviolability and sanctity of human life preclude sanctioning any form of intervention with the human body, even for the purpose of finding a cure for a disease, unless it is believed that there is a real possibility that the patient subjected to the experimental procedure might directly benefit from it. Without such a possibility, even the expectation that a given procedure will contribute to medical progress, which will benefit humanity, cannot justify causing suffering to individuals, who, as creatures bearing the image of God, are inviolable and must not be used as guinea pigs. While there are halakhic opinions permitting a patient to give his consent even to life-threatening procedures such as donation of a kidney on the ground that an individual may endanger his own life to save the life of another human being,[42] it is questionable whether such permission may be granted in cases when the potential benefit accruing to others is merely a matter of speculation. There is a crucial distinction to be drawn between permitting an individual to undergo risky procedures when there is a high probability that it will redound to the benefit of another patient versus sanctioning experimentation when there is only a remote chance that another person will actually derive benefit from it.

IV

Various laws pertaining to charitable giving and the performance of acts of lovingkindness offer additional evidence that Jewish ethics involves responsiveness to concerns transcending social utilitarianism. The commandment "Love thy neighbor as thyself" mandates concern for the individual *qua* individual, even in situations where the performance of a particular philanthropic act would decrease rather than increase the total aggregate of social utility.

While, generally, helping the needy enhances the collective well-being of society and could be justified on the basis of social utility, talmudic law also mandates philanthropic acts for which considerations of social justice or utility cannot be invoked. For instance, according to Jewish law, the obligation to help an individual to obtain "what he lacks"[43] is not determined by objective standards but by individual circumstances. Responding to this norm, Hillel went so far as to serve as a footman to someone who, due to financial reverses, could no longer afford the life style to which he had been accustomed.[44] Hillel reasoned that since true philanthropy reflects concern for the particular needs of an individual and not only for the collective well-being of society, it was his duty to provide the kind of luxury to which this individual had become accustomed.

Hillel's self-sacrificing actions would hardly be warranted by considerations of social utility. But far from being identical with Mill's general welfare principle, the love commandment mandates that we respond to the particular needs of individuals *qua* individuals, who because of their own unique history may have special requirements. One of the objectives of Jewish ethics is the cultivation of the spiritual vision and sensitivity to perceive of such needs, the satisfaction of which, from a strictly utilitarian point of view, will not necessarily maximize the general welfare.

The kind of benevolence displayed by Hillel makes sense only if we assume that the practice of lovingkindness should be inspired not merely by the requirements of a just society, which meets the needs of the underprivileged, but also by the religious demand to engage in altruistic actions for their own sake. The commandment to "love thy neighbor as thyself" goes beyond the ethical requirement of helping to increase the total welfare of society and to participate in *yishuv ha'olam* (the settlement of the world), because it applies even in situations when the fulfillment of this commandment would actually result in reduced pleasure for society.

Rabbi Mosheh Tzvi Neriah has called attention to an interesting distinction between two types of charitable giving:[45] (1) assistance rendered to the underprivileged, which is mandated out of concern for the general well-being of society, whose interests are best served when the basic needs of its marginal members are satisfied, versus (2) assistance provided out of genuine altruism and concern for an individual *qua* individual. Whereas the former represents a universal moral obligation, the latter is a special feature of Jewish ethics, which obligates only those subject to the provisions of the Sinaitic Covenant.

The obligation to care for a fellow human being is an exclusively biblical notion. Greek ethics restricted the domain of moral virtues to those dispositions and acts as were deemed conducive to the self-realization and self-fulfillment of individuals. Morality was regarded as an important means to develop human beings who are qualified to function properly within human society. There was, however, no concept of caring for another person for altruistic reasons. Such an obligation existed only if one were bound to another person by special bonds of friendship or when concern for the welfare of others would insure the stability of society, without which individuals could not flourish. Because genuine altruism had its roots in the Bible, medieval Christian writers treated charity not as a cardinal but as a purely theological virtue. More recently, Nietzsche went so far as to denounce Judaism for subverting what he regarded as proper moral standards by introducing to Western civilization such notions as concern for the weak, the underprivileged, and the oppressed, which he denounced as unhealthy manifestations of a "slave morality."

But while it is highly appealing to us as Jews to claim a historical connection between biblical religion and the rise of altruism, we would be guilty of the "genetic fallacy" were we to argue that religious ethics alone can provide a foundation for genuine philanthropy and altruism. Religion cannot claim a monopoly on inspiring humanitarian sentiments. Even without any kind of religious underpinnings, individuals or societies may be capable of cultivating what Professor Nozick has labeled "pull morality,"[46] which in contrast with "push morality" regards the well-being of the other as an end in itself and not merely as a means to further one's own interests.

Indeed, it is quite feasible that a purely secular morality could engender the notion of welfare rights based solely upon considerations of social justice. But, without a religious foundation demanding the performance of acts of lovingkindness, it would be absurd to advocate that one follow Hillel's example and serve as a footman to a member of the aristocracy who has become impoverished.[47]

In an incisive study,[48] R. Aharon Lichtenstein has pointed out that at times the obligations of personal ethics do not merely extend beyond the requirements mandated by concern for the maximum benefit of society, but there are cases when personal moral duties actually demand performance of actions that run counter to the interests of society. In the words of the Sages, the value of a charitable gift depends upon the amount of *chesed* invested in it rather than that of the objective good that has been accomplished.[49]

That the performance of acts of benevolence should be welcomed as opportunities to fulfill the religious requirement to emulate divine benevolence is graphically illustrated in a much-quoted Aggadah. It relates that Abraham was in anguish because he could not spot any travelers who required his hospitality.[50] Far from rejoicing that nobody needed his assistance, he actually bemoaned his lack of opportunity to practice philanthropy.

Professor Twersky has pointed out that Maimonides, for all his emphasis upon the social utility of philanthropy, at times classifies philanthropic acts not as commandments between man and his fellow-man but as commandments between man and God.[51] While most of the discussion of this issue has to be reserved for the next chapter, on agent-morality, it must be observed at this point that, according to Maimonides, philanthropy should be viewed from two different perspectives. On the one hand, it serves to alleviate the needs of the recipient. On the other hand, performing philanthropic acts is a boon to the benefactor, who derives spiritual benefits from fulfilling his religious obligations. As Samson R. Hirsch put it so felicitously, the performance of acts of lovingkindness is man's "holiest and most God-like task."[52] In the Maimonidean system, the practice of lovingkindness, apart from its intrinsic significance, functions as an important means in the quest for self-perfection in keeping with the religious ideal of *imitatio dei*.

The realization that moral actions and virtues have a dual purpose enables us to dispose of what initially seems to be a self-contradiction in the concluding chapter of the *Guide*. At first, Maimonides denies moral perfection the status of an intrinsic value:

> This species of perfection is likewise a preparation for something else and not an end in itself. For all moral habits are concerned with what occurs between a human individual and someone else. This perfection regarding moral habits is, as it were, the disposition to be useful to people; consequently it is an instrument for someone else. For if you suppose a human individual is alone, acting on no one, you will find that all his moral virtues are in vain and without employment and unneeded, and that they do not perfect the individual in anything; for he only needs them . . . in regard to someone else.[53]

Despite this unequivocal assertion that moral perfection possesses only a relatively low status, Maimonides at the very end of the chapter makes the startling declaration that we reach supreme religious perfection through the cultivation of the thirteen ethical attributes, which, according to the Torah,[54] characterize the ways of God.[55] The difficulty, however, can be resolved when we take into account that moral perfection serves two distinct functions. It can be regarded simply as an instrumental value — a means to promote socially beneficial conduct. But it can also be regarded as an intrinsic value, the highest level of which can be reached only by individuals who have risen to a height of moral and intellectual perfection that enables them to attain the intellectual apprehension of God. At this stage, moral perfection ceases to be a purely social desideratum but instead represents the realization of the ultimate religious ideal of *imitatio dei* — the *summum bonum* of the individual.

It is, however, imperative to reiterate that the primary objective of philanthropy is to alleviate the suffering of a fellow human being—not to provide the benefactor with opportunities for spiritual growth. The giving of charity must not be viewed as a means towards the attainment of our own moral perfection, but as an activity intended to benefit another person.

The focus upon helping the beneficiary explains why Judaism has been perfectly willing to use coercive measures to obtain funds needed to provide for the indigent.[56] Charity is not merely a private virtue, but also a public responsibility. Moreover, unless a charitable gift is motivated by totally base sentiments such as the desire to humiliate the recipient,[57] even a purely selfish motive will not render the charitable gift worthless. According to the Talmud, "If someone declares, 'I donate a sela [a sum of money] to charity in order that my child may live' . . . he is regarded as a perfectly righteous individual."[58] Similarly, the Rabbis encouraged contributing tithes even when such giving is intended as an investment, because it is motivated by the expectation that the performance of the good deed will be rewarded with wealth.[59] As far as charity was concerned, the Rabbis placed far less importance upon the purity of the motive than they did with other religious duties, because what mattered to them above all was that the needy would receive proper help.[60]

CHAPTER FIVE

Act-Morality & Agent-Morality

IT HAS OFTEN BEEN SAID THAT JUDAISM IS NOT A creed but a religion of deeds. While this characterization contains an element of truth, it also gives rise to the misconception that Judaism addresses itself only to the regulation of overt conduct and is totally indifferent to the inner spiritual life — the realm of beliefs, states of minds, dispositions, or attitudes. My analysis of Maimonides' ethical views in this chapter demonstrates that Judaism is concerned not merely with what an agent does (act-morality) but also with what kind of person one *is* (agent-morality).

Much of the blame for this misunderstanding of Judaism rests with the uncritical acceptance of what amounted to a caricature of Judaism in the writings of Kant. His views were molded by early Christian polemical writings, which branded Judaism a legalism without any religious significance. Kant did not merely hail Christianity as a superior faith but went so far as to altogether deny Judaism the status of a religion, relegating it to a legal code completely devoid of spiritual value. Undoubtedly, Spinoza and Mendelssohn also bear considerable responsibility for Kant's failure to appreciate Judaism. Both these well-known Jews had contended that Judaism was not a religion but a legal system designed to regulate the conduct of the Jewish community.

This position, in extreme form, has been echoed by exponents of "Orthopraxis,"[1] who argue that theoretical beliefs, dispositions, and attitudes play no role within normative Judaism. In their opinion, Halakhah allegedly does not mandate belief in dogmas but is concerned exclusively with overt behavior. It was in opposition to this widely held view that Abraham Joshua Heschel time and again inveighed against what he termed "Pan-Halakhism," which, he complained, amounted to the reduction of Judaism to a "religious behaviorism."[2]

I

While it cannot be denied that regulation of conduct is one of the most salient features of Judaism, Jewish religious law relates not only to the realm of actions but also encompasses beliefs and dispositions. Unlike civil law, which depends upon societal sanctions to secure compliance and can therefore only deal with overt conduct, divine law can also address itself to those states of mind and dispositions that do not manifest themselves in observable behavior. In the words of the Book of Samuel: "Man looks at the outward appearance, but God looks at the heart."[3] Since divine law does not require human sanctions to secure compliance, the Torah dictates norms governing states of mind such as "Thou shalt not covet,"[4] "Thou shalt not hate thy brother in thy heart,"[5] or "Thou shalt love thy neighbor as thyself."[6]

To be sure, the question remains whether it is possible to legislate sentiments or attitudes. Human beings can exercise control only over their conduct, not over their states of mind or dispositions. This was one of the reasons Kant insisted that any act motivated by sentiment or inclination cannot qualify as a moral act. In his view, only an action performed out of a sense of duty — that is, motivated by purely rational principles — can possess moral value.

Although the *possession* of states of mind or emotional attitudes cannot be objects even of divine legislation, it makes perfect sense to mandate the *cultivation* of desirable states of mind, be they intellectual beliefs or emotional dispositions. In his discussion of the Tenth Commandment, "Thou shalt not covet," Ibn Ezra notes that the cultivation of a proper faith in God will give rise to a set of fatalistic attitudes that will make it impossible to become envious of someone else's good fortune.[7]

This distinction between possessing and cultivating a state of mind can also dispose of difficulties presented by the Maimonidean interpretation of the First Commandment. According to Maimonides, the verse "I am the Lord thy God Who brought thee out of the land of Egypt, out of the house of bondage"[8] is not merely a preamble but an outright commandment, which mandates acquiring knowledge of the existence of God.[9] Crescas objected to the Maimonidean exegesis, arguing that belief in the existence of God cannot be the object of a commandment, since the very notion of a divine commandment already presupposes belief in the existence of God. Hence, according to Crescas, the first verse of the Decalogue cannot be treated as a commandment, but must be regarded as a preamble to the Commandments or as a presupposition of the Torah. But this objection can easily be disposed of if, following R. Joseph B. Soloveitchik's analysis,[10] we interpret the Maimonidean doctrine as ordaining not simply the acceptance of the belief in God but an ongoing effort to strengthen and deepen this belief.

It is in this light that we should view the highly original doctrine of Maimonides that the biblical verse, "Thou shalt walk in His ways" (Deuteronomy 28:9), is the basis of a specific religious obligation to develop virtuous traits of character.[11] The *cultivation* of virtues is not simply mandated as a means toward moral action, but constitutes an end in itself. Unlike R. Chaim Vital, who maintained that the cultivation of *middot* (virtuous dispositions) is not a specific mitzvah but is merely necessary as a prelude to the proper performance of *mitzvot*,[12] Maimonides regards virtuous dispositions as intrinsic rather than merely instrumental values. His ethical system does not limit itself to act-

morality—the moral propriety of particular actions—but focuses as well upon agent-morality—the moral quality of the
state of mind of the agent.

In his explanation of the commandment to cultivate proper
de'ot (virtuous dispositions), Maimonides adds the qualification
"according to one's ability."[13] Since the attainment of divine
moral perfection is beyond human capacity, it is incumbent
upon all individuals to strive continuously to perfect their traits
of character in response to the religious imperative to imitate
the ways of God.

In one of his earliest works, his Commentary on the Mishnah,
Maimonides notes that whereas the ideal performance of purely
ritual commandments involves struggling against our contrary
inclinations, in accordance with the principle that "the reward
is proportionate to the effort,"[14] this maxim does not apply to
the realm of ethical conduct. Here the situation is altogether
different. One reaches the highest rung of moral development
when the performance of moral actions reflects one's moral nature and, therefore, no longer requires any battle against inclinations.[15] Accordingly, benevolent acts are more meritorious if inspired by kindness rather than performed simply to discharge a
religious duty. For Maimonides, the ethico-religious ideal stipu-
lates that moral actions not merely conform to the requirements
of benevolence and justice, but reflect the virtuous disposition
of the agent.[16]

It has been argued that only because Maimonides had assimi-
lated Greek philosophical doctrines did he find it necessary to
make a radical distinction between motivations recommended
for ethical commandments and those most desirable for ritual
commandments.[17] Indeed, at first blush, it would appear that he
was simply echoing the Aristotelian doctrine, according to
which virtue is acquired through performing actions required
by virtue.[18] A conception of ethics based upon the attainment
of excellence as its ultimate objective seems to reflect the spirit
of the basically egotistical thrust characteristic of Greek morality
(what Professor Nozick terms "push morality"[19]) rather than the

other-regarding thrust of biblical morality (Nozick's "pull morality").

Although Maimonides could not completely escape Aristotelian influences, his doctrine of virtue is grounded not in Greek ethical or metaphysical thought, but represents a highly original, yet thoroughly Jewish religious approach. Unlike Aristotle, Maimonides advocates cultivating the virtues not for metaphysical reasons (self-realization in keeping with the requirements of human nature) or in the pursuit of happiness (without excellent traits of character one cannot enjoy the sense of well-being that is derived from proper functioning of one's faculties), but in response to the religious norm of "Thou shalt walk in His ways." He interprets this commandment, in accordance with the *Sifrei*,[20] as mandating the cultivation of such dispositions as graciousness, compassion, holiness, and other positive qualities.

> As He is called gracious, you too be gracious; just as He is called merciful, you too be merciful; just as He is called holy, you too be holy.[21]

After paraphrasing this Rabbinic text, Maimonides continues with his own formulation:

> In like manner the prophets applied all these terms to God: slow to anger and abundant in loving-kindness, just and righteous, perfect, powerful, strong, and the like. They did so to proclaim that these ways are good and right, and a man is obliged to train himself to follow them and to imitate them according to his strength.[22]

In this formulation Maimonides completely disregards the Babylonian Talmud's exegesis of the biblical verse "after the Lord your God ye shall walk" (Deuteronomy 13:5), which in the tractate Sotah is treated as a reference to the *practice* of lovingkindness.

> As He clothes the naked, so you too shall clothe the naked; . . . as He visits the sick, you too shall visit the sick; . . . as He consoles the mourners, you too shall console the mourners; . . . as He buries the dead, you too shall bury the dead.[23]

In his *Sefer Ha-Mitzvot,* which was intended as a preliminary work to his *Code,* Maimonides draws upon this talmudic source as well as the above-quoted *Sifrei* to point out that the commandment "Thou shalt walk in His ways" refers *both* to the performance of benevolent actions and the cultivation of moral dispositions. In his later and more authoritative *magnum opus,* the *Mishneh Torah,* he restricts the import of the commandment to the cultivation of moral dispositions.

It is puzzling that Maimonides not only relies upon a less authoritative Rabbinic source (*Sifrei* rather than the Babylonian Talmud) to explain the commandment "Thou shalt walk in His ways," but cites as an explanation of this commandment a text from the *Sifrei,* which has no connection whatsoever with the verse that he invokes as prooftext for the commandment to cultivate moral virtues. Actually, the *Sifrei* passage refers to a biblical verse that states a promise rather than a commandment: "For if you diligently keep all this commandment which I command you, to do it, to love the Lord thy God, to walk in His ways, and to cleave to Him" (Deuteronomy 11:22), *not* to the verse "Thou shalt walk in His ways" (Deuteronomy 28:9), which may be interpreted as a commandment and which in the Maimonidean scheme serves as the source of the obligation to perfect one's character.

Despite difficulties posed by his unconventional use of Rabbinic sources, there is a rather simple explanation why Maimonides abandoned his early position as formulated in the *Sefer Ha-Mitzvot* and limited the range of applicability of "Thou shalt walk in His ways" to cultivating virtues. As his views matured, he felt constrained to guard against the misconception that cultivating moral virtues was an instrumental rather than an intrinsic value. For Maimonides, the reverse held true. Moral actions, apart from their intrinsic merits, also function as stepping stones to the attainment of moral virtue. He therefore found it necessary to point out that while the performance of altruistic actions is grounded in "Love thy neighbor as thyself," the commandment "Thou shalt walk in His ways" refers exclusively to the cultivation of dispositions as an end in itself, without any reference whatsoever to act-morality.[24]

Adopting the Aristotelian view that the performance of moral actions is a means to the cultivation of virtue, he recommends giving small amounts of charity on many occasions rather than one large gift. The repeated performance of acts of charity, however insignificant, will do more to cultivate a charitable disposition in the donor than giving one major gift, even though such a gift would be a tremendous boon to the recipient.[25]

It is instructive that Maimonides places the section dealing with the cultivation of moral dispositions (that is, agent-morality) at the very beginning of the *Code*,[26] immediately following the discussion of the most fundamental principles of an individual's relationship to God, such as belief in monotheism and prophecy, the love and fear of God, free will and repentance, and so forth, whereas the discussion of various facets of act-morality such as the obligation to perform acts of charity, justice, and benevolence is reserved for later parts of the *Code*, such as *Hilkhot Matnot Ani'im* and *Hilkhot Avel*, which deal with interpersonal relations. Furthermore, in the last sentence of the opening chapter of *Hilkhot De'ot*, Maimonides calls attention to the personal rather than the social benefits ensuing from cultivating the proper traits of character. "He who walks in this way brings good and blessing upon himself."[27]

Since the commandment "Love thy neighbor as thyself" is included both in *Hilkhot De'ot* and in *Hilkhot Avel*, it seems likely that this particular commandment has a twofold function: (1) insofar as *Hilkhot De'ot* is concerned, love of our fellow man is one of the vital components of an agent's moral excellence; (2) in *Hilkhot Avel*, however, the performance of *acts* of lovingkindness to our fellow human beings is mandated because of the benefits accruing to the beneficiary rather than to the benefactor. Significantly, since *Hilkhot De'ot* focuses on agent-morality, the commandments listed in this section are viewed not as socially useful ordinances but as instrumentalities to help us develop virtuous dispositions. *Hilkhot Avel*, on the other hand, serves an entirely different purpose. It deals with social ethics and inter-personal relationships. The love commandment is formulated here not as an aspect of virtue-ethics but as the ultimate source of the obligation to perform benevolent *acts*.

Awareness of the twofold significance of the love command-ment enables us to understand seeming discrepancies in Mai-monides' formulation. Whereas in *Hilkhot De'ot* the command-ment mandates that we love *every* Jew as ourselves, an important qualification is added in *Hilkhot Avel*. We are obligated to love only those who "share our commitment to Torah and *mitzvot*." The simplest way to resolve this difficulty is by taking account of the context of the respective formulations. On the one hand, only those who share commitment to Torah and *mitzvot* are entitled to receive the help mandated by the love command-ment. But, on the other hand, to guard themselves against be-coming callous or self-centered, agents must cultivate senti-ments of love even toward those Israelites who do not share their religious commitments.[28]

Furthermore, although the love imperative governing actions is restricted to helping Jews, agent-morality, as noted previously in chapter 3, dictates that philanthropic assistance be extended to non-Jews as well. In contradistinction to many other authori-ties, Maimonides interprets the talmudic requirement to prac-tice philanthropy in our relations to non-Jews not as a counsel of expediency based upon self-interest but as a moral imperative reflecting the dictates of agent-morality.[29]

II

Why does agent-morality play such a pivotal role in Maimoni-dean ethics, and not in other Jewish ethical systems?[30] One of the most salient features of Maimonides' entire system is the emphasis placed upon attaining proper states of mind, even when they do not affect matters of conduct. As mentioned pre-viously, Maimonides regarded the deepening of one's intellec-tual awareness of God, not merely one's belief in Him, as an outright commandment. Moreover, he found it necessary to formulate thirteen articles of faith, because, in his opinion, observing the commandments alone, unless accompanied by at least a rudimentary familiarity with the basic intellectual tenets of Judaism, would not make one eligible for a share in the world-to-come. He even elevated belief in the non-corporeal nature of God into a dogma.[31] Since Maimonides attaches such great weight to proper states of mind, even if they do not impinge upon matters of conduct, it is not surprising that he should consider cultivation of the proper traits of character (*de'ot*) of primary importance.

That Maimonides was fully aware of the originality of his approach to virtue-ethics is attested by the fact that in the "Laws of Repentance"[32] he engages in an extensive polemic against the opinion that repentance is required only for sins involving conduct and emphatically declares that, because evil traits of character pose a far greater peril to our spiritual well-being than do evil actions, it is imperative we confess and seek to amend flaws in our character.[33]

The importance Maimonides attached to the cultivation of desirable traits of character was a pioneering breakthrough in Jewish ethics. His originality can also be seen in his treatment of the biblical passage "and thou shalt cleave to Him."[34] Although he seemingly merely paraphrases the Rabbinic interpretation that mandates attachment to scholars of the Law,[35] he actually re-interprets it by adding the phrase "so that we should learn from their actions."[36] There is no basis whatsoever in the Rabbinic sources that attachment to scholars of the Law is mandated in order to provide us with role models. One could interpret the intention of the Rabbinic text, which mandates that we help scholars of the Law to earn a living or to marry their children, that through such respectful treatment of *talmidei chakhamim* we express reverence for God and His Torah. But for Maimonides the purpose of the attachment to scholars is educational. We should associate with them so that through imitation we learn to develop desirable traits of character.[37]

As pointed out previously in chapter 1 the placement of this commandment in *Hilkhot De'ot* rather than in *Hilkhot Talmud Torah*, the natural locus for a discussion of the role of scholars and our obligations toward them, illustrates a distinctive feature of the Maimonidean ethical system. There is no way to define the various desirable traits of character. Just as Aristotle insisted that the "golden mean" can only be described by pointing to the dispositions exhibited by individuals renowned for the excellence of their practical wisdom, so, too, Maimonides maintains that it is only the model of the *Talmid Chakham* that can provide us with an understanding of what constitute proper traits of character.

Maimonides' treatment of prophecy furnishes additional evidence of the vital role that cultivation of an ethical personality plays in his system. In marked contrast with many other Jewish thinkers who viewed prophecy primarily as a faculty granted to certain individuals to enable them to fulfill socially beneficial missions, Maimonides emphasizes that prophecy is not a gratuitous gift, but an achievement. Only those who have achieved the highest possible level of religious perfection are eligible. To be sure, God may *withhold* prophecy even from qualified individuals. But He will not confer it, unless the necessary moral and intellectual perfections have been attained. That Maimonides discusses the qualifications for prophecy in his ethical treatise, the Introduction to *Pirkei Avot,* shows that for him striving to become worthy of prophecy represents the ultimate religious aspiration.[38]

For Maimonides, one becomes eligible for prophecy not so much because of the quality of one's actions but because of the excellence of one's intellectual and moral virtues, such as wisdom, generosity, temperance, and such total preoccupation with lofty intellectual pursuits as to become uninterested in the trivial pursuits of ordinary individuals.[39] On the other hand, "vices such as lust, arrogance, irascibility, rage, impudence, love of money . . . are veils separating man from God"[40] and preclude the attainment of prophetic status.

For all the novelty of the Maimonidean conception of virtue-ethics, there exist earlier Aggadic sources, which treat the cultivation of moral dispositions as a religious imperative. The Tanna Abba Sha'ul, for example, commenting on the verse, "This is my God and I shall build Him an abode,"[41] notes: "Be like Him. As He is gracious and compassionate, you be gracious and compassionate." Rashi, in his commentary to the Talmud, suggests that Abba Sha'ul was here interpreting the Hebrew *ve'anveihu* in the sense of *ani ve'Hu* (I and He). Or, to quote Rashi's own words: "I shall make myself like Him and cling to His ways." Similarly, *Sifra*[42] associates Abba Sha'ul's emphasis upon emulating divine moral perfection with a comment on the biblical verse "Ye shall be holy, because I, the Lord your God, am holy."[43] In this reading, Abba Sha'ul treats the quest for moral perfection as an aspect of *imitatio dei*.

This particular source directly and explicitly links moral virtues with *imitatio dei*. Many other biblical and Rabbinic texts, without linking the acquisition of desirable traits of character with the imitation of God, similarly dwell upon the importance of character traits such as holiness, righteousness, saintliness, humility, compassion, and so on.[44] Greek philosophy certainly had no monopoly on the concept of virtue. As a matter of fact, the Talmud regards the possession of such virtues as compassion, sensitivity, and benevolence as the very hallmarks of Jewish identity.[45] There is even an opinion that an individual lacking compassion cannot possibly qualify as a descendant of the Patriarch Abraham.[46]

It might be argued that these sources do not conclusively demonstrate that moral dispositions constitute an intrinsic value, but rather that their cultivation might serve the solely *instrumental* function of promoting moral conduct. Charitable persons, for example, are far more likely than self-centered individuals to respond to the needs of the indigent. One might, therefore, maintain that, in keeping with the principle, "the reward is proportionate to the effort,"[47] when ungenerous individuals succeed in overcoming their selfish nature and act charitably, such conduct, because it results from the suppression of natural inclinations, possesses even greater religious worth than acts of charity of generous persons, who perform such acts with relatively little effort.[48]

To be sure, traditional sources stressing the importance of

character traits need not necessarily be interpreted to lend support to Maimonides' position on the intrinsic value of desirable dispositions. Be that as it may, for Maimonides, the cultivation of moral dispositions is the only way in which human beings can engage in the "imitation of God."[49] Whereas Aristotle regarded contemplation as man's most God-like activity, Maimonides insists that man cannot imitate God at all; strictly speaking, only "the ways of God" can function as models in our quest for moral perfection, the attainment of which, when based upon intellectual perfection, represents the highest level of piety, the very acme of the religious ideal.[50]

Maimonides' emphasis upon the imitation of divine moral attributes explains why he finds it necessary to create a separate category—that is, the "attributes of action"—to supplement his doctrine of "negative attributes," which he developed because of his insistence that the absolute Oneness, Uniqueness, and Unity of God make it impossible to ascribe to Him any property. Why did he not simplify his system by interpreting both metaphysical and moral attributes of God as "negative attributes"? Had his sole concern been to reconcile the biblical attributes of God with his doctrine of His utter unknowability, then there really would have been no need for a separate category called "attributes of action." The most plausible explanation for this seemingly unnecessary complication seems to be that, in the Maimonidean system, the "attributes of action" were indispensable, because the divine moral attributes were to serve as the exemplars of moral perfection. Had Maimonides resorted to a purely negative interpretation of the divine moral attributes as he did for God's metaphysical properties, they could not possibly function as models for our own ethical life.[51]

III

Although Maimonides emphasizes that virtuous dispositions are engendered by virtuous conduct, he maintains that the higher rungs of ethico-religious development cannot be reached by moral conduct alone, but presuppose intellectual attainments. While mere obedience to the ethical rules prescribed by the Torah helps form virtuous dispositions, for Maimonides it is the cultivation of the intellect that leads to the higher levels of ethics ("the ethics of the pious," in his terminology). High standards of intellectual perfection enable us to apprehend the requirements of "the ethics of the pious." The latter includes appreciation of the need to go beyond the minimal ethical requirements and engage in supererogatory conduct and, at the highest stage of development, to perform moral action without any regard for self-interest.

That ethical perfection presupposes not merely knowledge and observance of ethical rules but also vision, sensitivity and responsibility — the ability to *respond* appropriately to the ethical imperatives of particular situations — becomes evident in the Maimonidean approach to supererogation. Contrast his approach with that of Nachmanides. The latter derived the obligation of going beyond the strict limits of the law and engaging in supererogatory conduct from the verse "Thou shalt do the right and the good."[52]

Maimonides, on the other hand, finds it impossible to treat supererogation as a paralegal obligation. Since he takes it for granted that laws must be general and universally applicable, he cannot include imperatives addressed exclusively to a spiritual elite under the category of law. Maimonides never refers to a religious prescription that mandates supererogatory conduct. Instead, whenever supererogation is mentioned in his *Code,* he employs the description "he who acts beyond the requirements of the law." For Maimonides, there exists no commandment to perform supererogatory actions. Supererogation is only indirectly related to the law, because the capacity to apprehend supererogatory requirements is a by-product of spiritual perfection, which is only attained when individuals, in response to the commandment "Thou shalt walk in His ways," reach the higher levels of ethical sensitivity at which they are no longer content to abide by the minimal standards of the law.

Another feature of ethico-religious perfection, according to Maimonides, is the attainment of totally selfless motivation in carrying out religious obligations and striving for ideals. In his view, even the hope for spiritual rewards in the hereafter detracts from the purity of one's religious motives. One qualifies for "serving God out of love" only when self-regarding motives cease to be factors in one's religious life.[53]

As mentioned previously in chapter 4, most other Jewish philosophers do not share Maimonides' attitude. They maintain that though, ideally, expectation of material rewards should not be a factor inspiring religious piety, the anticipation of spiritual rewards is perfectly acceptable as an incentive for piety. Saadiah, for example, contends that human beings should obey divine commandments in order to achieve the very purpose of all creation. In his anthropocentric scheme, God's purpose in creating the universe was to make it possible for human beings to earn the supreme bliss of the hereafter.[54] Isaac Arama goes even further and insists that one cannot properly perform a divine commandment, unless one is confident that a mitzvah engenders a spiritual reward. He adopts an approach antithetical to that of Maimonides, who saw in the Rabbinic dictum "The reward of a mitzvah is a mitzvah"[55] support for his position that the performance of a mitzvah tends to refine the religious sensibilities and character of an individual, rendering the performance of another mitzvah less difficult. For Arama, however, awareness of the ensuing spiritual reward forms an integral part of the proper performance of a mitzvah.[56]

There is a simple explanation why Maimonides, in seeming conflict with the biblical assertion that the commandments were ordained for the benefit of human beings, attaches such weight to the doctrine that the service of God should be performed without being tainted by any self-interest, however noble. As mentioned previously, for Maimonides, cultivation of moral dispositions was not mandated by eudaimonistic (concern for happiness) or metaphysical considerations reflecting the requirements of human nature. Maimonides was a religious Jew, not a Greek philosopher. For him, the obligation to cultivate virtues was derived from the *religious* imperative to imitate the ways of God. Since God's love for His creatures is totally other-regarding and untainted by selfish motives, the imitation of God logically calls for whole-hearted efforts to divest oneself of concerns of self-interest in the attempt to reach the highest level of religious perfection, in which all one's actions are performed for the sake of God.[57]

That Maimonidean virtue-ethics is grounded in *imitatio dei* rather than in the requirements of human nature profoundly affects his account of what constitute desirable traits of character. In his earliest writings, Maimonides treated virtues simply as the requirements of psychological well-being. He condoned deviations from the middle road only when extremes were necessary as temporary expedients to correct imbalances. Just as one must straighten out a bent twig by bending it in the other direction, so, too, in order to achieve the ideal of the golden mean, one must sometimes aim temporarily for the opposite extreme to overcome excess or deficiency. At the time of the writing of the *Mishnah Commentary,* Maimonides extolled the middle road as *the* ethical ideal. He did follow Aristotle, however, in allowing for some exceptions to this general rule. According to the *Nicomachean Ethics,* in some cases (for example, spite, shamelessness, envy, and so on.) the mean is completely unacceptable, because the disposition is in itself bad.[58] For that matter, in the Aristotelian conception, proper dispositions do not always represent the mathematical midpoints between extremes. Yet even at this early stage, Maimonides, because of his theocentric orientation, parted company with Aristotle on important details and insisted that insofar as pride and anger are concerned, the middle way must be eschewed altogether; only the extremes of humility and total lack of irascibility constitute desirable dispositions.[59] Whereas Aristotle admires the proud man, who represented the mean between the humble and the vain man, and conversely looked upon disdain for worldly honor as a vice, Maimonides regards a total absence of desire for honor, acclaim, or fame as a moral ideal.[60] The numerous condemnations of the sin of pride and the frequent references in classical rabbinical literature[61] to anger as the equivalent of idolatry left Maimonides no alternative but to reject the positive Aristotelian attitude toward pride and anger.

A remarkable shift, however, in Maimonides' overall approach to virtue occurred in his later and more authoritative *magnum opus,* the *Mishneh Torah.* He no longer advocates the cultivation of the proper virtues simply as a prescription for mental health, which possesses religious value to the extent that it is pursued for the sake of God. At this more advanced stage in the evolution of Maimonidean virtue-ethics, cultivation of virtue is transformed into an outright religious imperative. Going to an extreme is no longer merely condoned as a corrective, but is extolled as the "ethics of the pious," which goes beyond the less rigorous demands of the "ethics of the middle road."

But there still remains a difficulty with respect to the interpretation of Maimonides' position on virtues as set forth in his *Code.* In the first chapter of *Hilkhot De'ot,* Maimonides advocates cultivating the middle road rather than "the way of the pious" (supererogation) in order to imitate the "ways of God";[62] but in the second chapter, he extols the extremist "ethics of the pious" as the superior religious ideal. Moreover, in the second chapter, humility, defined as the midpoint between pride and total self-effacement, is rejected as unsatisfactory; Maimonides instead recommends the cultivation of total self-effacement: "The good way is not that a man may be merely humble, but that he have a lowly spirit, that his spirit be very submissive."[63] Similarly, whereas in the first chapter, the "ways of the wise" dictate that "one only become angry about a large matter that deserves anger so that something like it not be done again,"[64] the second chapter mandates that one should condition oneself "not to be angry even for something it is proper to be angry about."[65] Accordingly, it is the hallmark of the righteous "to be insulted but not to insult; to hear themselves reviled and do not reply; they act out of love and rejoice in afflictions."[66]

There is a vast literature dealing with the seeming contradictions between the first two chapters of *Hilkhot De'ot.* Hermann Cohen maintained that the ethics of the middle road, as formulated in the first chapter, must be viewed as mere counsels of prudence that fail to satisfy the higher requirements of a religious ethics inspired by the quest for *imitatio dei.* According to

Cohen, these religiously inferior strata of Maimonidean ethics represent "survivals" of an Aristotelian prudential ethics, which should be overcome and transcended in the quest for religious ideals. Shimon Rawidowicz, however, categorically rejects this solution.[67] He contends that the "ethics of the middle road" cannot be dismissed simply as the intrusions of Greek elements into biblical morality, because Maimonides explicitly asserts that adopting the "middle road" fulfills the commandment "Thou shalt walk in His ways."

I have elsewhere[68] attempted to demonstrate that the advocacy of moderation, characteristic of the "middle of the road" approach (defined by Maimonides as "the ways of the wise") reflects the traditional requirements of *yishuv ha'olam*[69] (rendering the world fit for human habitation). This ethical approach, however, also transcends prudential utilitarian concerns and represents *one* of the modes of *imitatio dei*. The Talmud attaches enormous religious significance to whatever activities contribute to *yishuv ha'olam*. Thus, for example, in the opinion of Rav Sheshet, a Babylonian Amora, a professional gambler is disqualified from serving as a witness because "he is not engaged in the settlement of the world."[70] For Maimonides, the cultivation of character traits needed for society to function properly acquires the status of a religious imperative, which obliges us to pattern ourselves after the model of the Creator. In my opinion, Maimonides, who has a penchant for unification, creates no dichotomy between a religious and a secular Aristotelian ethics. Instead, he operates with two distinct tiers of *religious* ethics — that is, an ethics of *yishuv ha'olam hazeh*[71] (settlement of this world) or *yishuv ha'aretz*[72] (settlement of the earth) on the one hand, and an "ethics of the pious," on the other — which remain in a perpetual state of tension with one another.

It is understandable why some thinkers tend to regard only the "ethics of the pious," with its focus upon humility, as a genuinely religious ethics. The various virtues of prudential ethics (the ethics of the wise equals the ethics of *yishuv ha'olam*) set forth in Chapter 1 of the "Laws concerning Character Traits" closely parallel various forms of secular ethics. On the other hand, the goal of total self-effacement (one of the major characteristics of the "ethics of the pious") has been condemned by Aristotle and later by Spinoza as being totally incompatible with the sense of self-worth and self-esteem that is vital for the proper functioning of human beings in society. Indeed, it is only within the context of a theocentric perspective, with its emphasis upon human beings' total dependence upon God, that extreme humility becomes a virtue.[73] As a matter of fact, kabbalistic ethics, especially as developed by Moses Cordovero in his *Tomer Devorah,* looked upon humility as the foundation for a variety of virtues and practices that he deemed indispensable to religious ethics. His ethics of altruism, forbearance, and forgiveness is entirely based upon the religious ideal of imitating various aspects of divine humility. It should thus be hardly surprising that Hermann Cohen and other Jewish thinkers were reluctant to endow with genuine religious significance what we previously defined as the ethics of *yishuv ha'olam.*

Steven Schwarzschild,[74] in his incisive discussion of this question, maintains that the "higher" ethics as developed by Maimonides in the second chapter represents an exposition of the ideal Messianic ethics meant to supersede the lower level of religious ethics of chapter 1,[75] which advocates the virtues of the golden mean. As against this interpretation, I contend that the dialectical tension between the two levels is unavoidable, because it arises out of the dialectical tensions characterizing the human condition. There is considerable internal evidence for my position. The very conclusion of the second chapter, for all its emphasis upon "the ethics of the pious," reverts to the requirement to follow the ethical mean. If the inferior "ethics of the wise" should ideally be completely superseded by the superior "ethics of the pious," such an ending to this chapter would hardly make sense.

My reading of Maimonides has been influenced by Rabbi Joseph B. Soloveitchik's ethico-religious views, especially as set forth in his essays, "The Lonely Man of Faith"[76] and "Majesty and Humility."[77] According to Rabbi Soloveitchik, human beings, on the one hand, are mandated to subdue the forces of nature for their own purposes. But, on the other hand, they must also be conscious of their limitations and recognize that their existential loneliness cannot be overcome by technological progress. There is need for a degree of withdrawal from the world in order to make possible the establishment of a Covenantal community with God.

Human dignity manifests itself in using reason and imagination to exercise dominion over the forces of nature. But the human condition also demands humility. Our sense of isolation can only be overcome through self-surrender and self-sacrifice to God.

We shall have occasion to return to this theme. But for our present purposes, it suffices to point out that once we postulate two distinct aspects of human nature standing in dialectical relationship, no ethics based upon such premises can be free of tensions. To be sure, these tensions give rise to difficulties. It is no simple task to satisfy the claims of two distinct ethical approaches, which at times make conflicting demands upon us. In any given existential situation, we cannot be certain whether to act in accordance with the standards of the "ethics of the wise" or those of the "ethics of the pious." But even without this added complication, the ethical domain is fraught with all sorts of ambiguities and dilemmas, which arise from the need to accommodate numerous conflicting values and principles. As unsatisfactory as it may be, we have no alternative but to rely upon admittedly fallible intuitions to guide us in making ethical decisions, especially when they involve highly delicate issues in agent-morality.

Since, unlike Cohen, Rawidowicz, and Schwarzschild, I do not treat the ethics of the wise as mere stepping stones to the higher ethics of the pious, I cannot look upon the latter as a utopian ethics. As long as we live in an unredeemed world, ethical decisions must be based upon realism, not upon the kind of action that would be appropriate under the ideal conditions of a totally redeemed Messianic world in which all evil has been overcome. It is for this reason that Judaism, despite its love of peace, categorically rejects pacifism. Non-resistance to evil, even when directed against one's own person, is not a saintly posture but an unconscionable moral wrong. We are duty-bound to resist aggression by force, if necessary, not only to protect other innocent victims, but also for self-protection. In our unredeemed world, we sometimes have no alternative but to choose between lesser and greater evils. From a Jewish perspective, it is morally preferable to choose the lesser evil—the killing of an aggressor—rather than the greater evil, allowing an aggressor to perpetrate violence against us.[78]

There is another reason why Maimonides' ethics of the pious cannot be interpreted in accordance with the kind of Messianic ethics advocated by Schwarzschild. Far from portraying the Messiah as a pacifist, Maimonides stresses that the Messiah, during the initial stages of the Redemption, will have to engage in warfare. Military victories are indispensable to establishing his authenticity as the "Messianic King." To advocate extreme pacifism as a requirement of Messianic ethics—as Hermann Cohen and Steven Schwarzschild did—is obviously a distortion of the Messianic idea as formulated by Maimonides, who included his discussion of the Messiah in the section of the *Code* originally entitled "Laws of Kings and Their Warfare."

The extremism espoused by Maimonides in chapter 2 of *Hilkhot De'ot,* provided that it be balanced by the ethics of *yishuv ha'olam* (chapter 1), is not at all an ethics of Messianism geared to the requirements of an ideal society; rather, Maimonides offers a thoroughly realistic ethical approach, which can guide human beings in the here-and-now of an unredeemed world, fraught with moral ambiguities and subject to strife and conflict.

CHAPTER SIX

Moral Dilemmas

T HE NEED TO ADJUDICATE THE CONFLICTING claims of "higher" and "lower" moralities points to one of the most difficult problems besetting ethics: the resolution of conflicts between competing principles, norms, and rules. Unlike most modern systems such as Kantian rationalism, social utilitarianism, or egotistical hedonism, which seek to justify all ethical norms by recourse to a single principle, Jewish Covenantal Ethics, as noted in chapter 1, does not suffer from such a monistic bias. Since Covenantal Ethics ultimately rests upon the foundation of a plurality of independent legal norms, broader general ethical principles play only a secondary role. No explicit, particular legal norm of the Halakhah can be set aside simply because it is perceived as contravening such general moral principles as "Love thy neighbor as thyself" or "Thou shalt do what is right and good."

Judaism operates with a pluralistic ethics that incorporates a variety of incommensurable values.[1] It, therefore, holds enormous potential for conflict between clashing norms. As a result, casuistry—the analysis and examination of the range of applicability of specific moral rules—emerges as one of the key features of Jewish ethical thought.[2] I am fully aware of the negative connotations of the term 'casuistry.' But I use this term deliberately, because any ethics containing specific rules or norms cannot avoid addressing the question as to what kind of *cases* are covered by a particular rule or law.

This holds especially true for an ethics that claims that its norms and ideals are grounded in Divine Revelation. It is logically impossible for a system of divine norms to be self-contradictory. Hence, a way must be found to resolve *apparent* conflicts. If, for example, in the case of a "white lie" we are confronted with a conflict between the requirements of truth-telling versus "the ways of peace," Jewish law resolves the dilemma through casuistry, restricting the imperative of truth-telling to those situations where obedience to this norm does not conflict with the higher obligation to promote peace. Unlike Kant, for whom truth-telling amounted to a categorical duty, Judaism sanctions telling an outright lie, in the interest of peace[3] or, for that matter, when truth-telling would lead to infractions of human dignity, modesty, or humility.[4] While both love (*chesed*) and truthfulness (*emet*) are divine moral attributes that are to be emulated, the former ranks higher because it represents the only moral property that, the Torah declares, God possesses *in abundance* (*rav chesed*).[5]

Because Jewish ethics assigns priority to benevolence, it employs casuistry to limit the range of applicability of truth- telling. Thus, according to some opinions, the formal prohibition against lying applies only to cases where deviation from the truth is intended to deceive another person and yield benefits to the liar at the expense of the victim.[6]

Deviations from the truth, which are prompted by considerations of self-interest, are unequivocally condemned. Failure to keep one's word in commercial transactions, even when the formalities required to make the agreements legally enforceable have not been fully complied with, warrants not merely moral condemnation but outright censure by a Jewish court.[7] Moreover, not only outright lies but even the concealment of relevant information or the creation of false impressions is strictly prohibited. Jewish law operates with such categories as *genevat da'at*[8] (the stealing of the mind) and *ona'at devarim* (wrong done by words). The former is the kind of misrepresentation that occurs,

> ... when one invites someone knowing that he will not accept, when one offers somebody gifts which one knows will not be accepted ... or when one mixes oil with vinegar.[9]

Similarly, the Mishnah states,

> It is prohibited to sell wine that was mixed with water, without informing the purchaser.[10]

A classic illustration of the prohibition against *ona'at devarim* is

> ... when one inquires, "How much does this item cost?" if one does not intend to purchase it.[11]

Misleading advertisements run afoul of the requirement of scrupulous honesty, which is demanded when deviation from the truth would cause harm to another individual. Judaism rejects the principle of *caveat emptor.* Instead, the vendor has a moral responsibility to inform the customer of defects. In the words of Maimonides,

> When one knows that there is some defect in one's merchandise, one must inform the purchaser. . . . One may not display old persons, animals or utensils that are for sale so that they appear young or new. But one may display new ones by polishing them . . . as required.[12]

Although mere failure to disclose all relevant available facts is regarded as a grievous offense, there are situations when deciding whether or not to tell the truth may confront us with perplexing moral ambiguities. On the one hand, Jewish religious law condemns *lashon hara* (maligning another person) even if the derogatory information is completely accurate and therefore does not entail any form of slander or libel. But there are many instances when, in order to protect another person from harm, it is necessary to convey negative information about someone. No simple rules enable us to determine whether sharing unfavorable information is prompted by a desire to be of help or whether it reflects the all-too-human tendency to gloat over the failings of others. We therefore have little choice but to rely upon our own ethical intuitions as to whether a particular situation warrants providing or suppressing unfavorable reports about someone else.

I

The sanctity of life is another moral principle that gives rise to serious ethical dilemmas. Jewish law maintains that, with the exception of the prohibitions of idolatry, murder, and sexual immorality, all norms and rules must be subordinated to the overriding imperative to preserve life.[13] There is universal consensus within Judaism that considerations of social utility do not warrant depriving individuals of their right to life. Active euthanasia can never be sanctioned. But not all questions involving sanctity versus quality of life can be resolved so easily. Although considerations about the quality of life are totally irrelevant when deciding whether to take any life, including one's own, they may play a crucial role in deciding questions relating to passive euthanasia. Jewish law recognizes a fundamental difference between the obligation not to kill and the obligation not to let die. In the opinion of many halakhic authorities, human intervention to prolong life is not required in situations when there is no hope for recovery and the extension of life would only increase the pain and suffering of the patient.[14]

What has been termed "life boat ethics" provides another example of how Jewish law, for all its insistence upon the absolute equality of the worth of all human life in the case of taking of life, allows for qualitative distinctions in assigning priorities for interventions designed to save lives. When it is impossible to save every life, some choice has to be made. This is why the Mishnah establishes specific guidelines for determining priorities in saving human lives.[15]

Similar considerations apply to the moral problems involving the practice of triage or the allocation of scarce resources for medical treatment. Obviously, as long as sufficient resources are available to meet all existing needs, concern for the sanctity of life obligates us to utilize the resources for the benefit of all patients, regardless of their social worth. Considerations of social utility play no role whatsoever in determining whether or not we are under moral obligation to extend the life of an individual. Hence, Jewish ethics is bound to repudiate the proposal that societal resources should not be expended for life-sustaining health care of the elderly.[16] Denying the elderly access to medical care, regardless of whether they can pay for it, would run counter to the absolute commitment to the sanctity of life that is the hallmark of Jewish ethics. It is only when there is no hope whatsoever for the patient's recovery and when withholding care will alleviate the suffering of the *patient* (not that of the family or of society at large) that we may be authorized to discontinue life-extending treatment.

There are situations, of course, when it is impossible to meet all medical needs and the denial of life-sustaining treatment to some individuals becomes unavoidable. As in "life boat ethics," some rational system of priorities should be devised rather than resorting to random selection of patients. As painful as it may be "to play God" and determine who shall live as the result of our intervention and who shall die as the consequence of our nonintervention, we cannot abdicate this responsibility. Random choice can hardly qualify as a more humane method to resolve our dilemmas. We simply cannot evade our awesome responsibility. After all, the decision to make a random choice is also a choice made by us and not one imposed upon us by forces beyond our control. However flawed or inadequate the criteria adopted, it still is preferable to make informed judgments than to rely on purely arbitrary methods. To be sure, it may turn out that, because of the variety of complex factors that have to be taken into consideration, even the employment of casuistry cannot provide definitive guidelines, and a certain amount of discretion must be vested in the individuals who are charged with the responsibility for making these painful decisions. Even reliance on subjective intuitions, which are at least based to some extent upon general principles, is still preferable to sheer randomness.

Casuistry also enables us to qualify the obligation to assign priority to saving our own lives. While as a general rule, Jewish law adopts Rabbi Akiva's view that "your own life takes precedence," and frowns upon sacrificing one's life in order to save others, Rabbi Kook permitted individuals to volunteer for suicide missions when carried out in the interest of the collective Jewish community. In other words, an act that would be illicit if performed to help individuals, would be legitimate if intended for the benefit of the community.[17]

While Rabbi Kook's ruling was not universally accepted, there are other cases where there is complete unanimity on the need to make a sharp distinction between personal and public interests. One of the most obvious examples is the Jewish attitude toward warfare, which Judaism allows, subject to various restrictions and limitations. As a matter of fact, Halakhah distinguishes between permissible, prescribed, and obligatory wars. But how can Judaism permit, in some instances even mandate, the waging of war, which is bound to endanger the lives of innocent individuals (such as young children) in the enemy camp, who could not by the wildest stretch of the imagination be perceived as aggressors? Does not warfare conflict with the well-established halakhic principle that one may not take the life of a nonaggressor to save one's own — a principle that is taken for granted by the Talmud on the basis of the "self-evident" proposition, "What makes you think that your blood is redder than that of your fellow human being?"[18]

This question cannot be answered by adopting a Machiavellian approach, which argues that moral standards apply only to individuals but not to states. The mere fact that Jewish law contains extensive regulations governing warfare is in itself conclusive evidence that the state is also bound by moral constraints. Even nontraditional thinkers such as Hermann Cohen,[19] Ahad Ha'am,[20] Martin Buber,[21] and Mordecai Kaplan[22] have argued that in Judaism many ethico-religious imperatives are addressed to the nation as a whole. Unlike Christianity, Judaism has never been prepared to accept the dichotomy between a secular and a religious realm. It has instead insisted that the political realm also conform to ethico-religious requirements. After all, when

Israel entered into the Sinaitic Covenant, it was for the explicit purpose of forming "a kingdom of priests and a holy people."[23]

Professor Whitehead's definition of religion as "what man does with his solitariness" may be appropriate for Christianity, but it does not do justice to Judaism. Whereas Christianity focuses upon the individual soul in relation to God, Judaism stresses personal responsibility for helping the people of Israel carry out its divine mission. Because Jews are related to God not only as individuals but also as members of a natural and historical community, an individual's identification, sense of kinship, and solidarity with all fellow Jews represents an indispensable ingredient of Jewish piety.[24] Maimonides brands as a heretic anyone who is indifferent to the welfare of the Jewish community.[25] One cannot adopt Judaism simply as a religious faith. Jewish conversion procedures involve assuming membership in the Jewish community of fate and faith. As Ruth put it, "Your people shall be my people and your God my God."[26]

Because of the communal thrust of Judaism, which assigns a religious mission to the nation, "my country, right or wrong," may represent good patriotism, but runs counter to the most basic tenets of Jewish morality. A religion that demands that we form a "holy people" could not possibly espouse the doctrine of *raisons d'état* to justify indiscriminately setting aside ethical norms when necessary for the public interest.

But it is one thing to argue that states as well as individuals are subject to moral constraints, and quite another to maintain that the same moral principles apply both to individuals and to collectivities. As Reinhold Niebuhr put it in his *Moral Man and Immoral Society,* states, unlike individuals, cannot be guided by ideals such as altruism, self-effacement, and humility. No statesman has a moral right to renounce the legitimate claims or forego the national interests of his own country for the sake of humanity at large. In a widely quoted essay,[27] Stuart Hampshire observed that ethics is not computational but operates with a plurality of incommensurable moral values. Judaism, thus, does not rule out warfare despite the fact that individuals would not be permitted to resort to similar actions; moral principles applicable to the body politic differ from those governing personal morality.

In a similar vein, Judaism mandates respect for the property of individuals and strictly prohibits any infringement on the rights of others. The Talmud even raises the question whether an individual may use someone else's property in order to save his own life. Yet no such limitations are placed upon properly constituted governmental authorities, who may levy taxes or expropriate property for the public good.[28] The Jewish religious tradition certainly does not subscribe to the Lockean thesis that the social contract limits the authority of the state to the protection of the natural rights of individuals.

So far we have in many instances resorted to casuistry to resolve dilemmas arising from the conflicts between moral norms. But there are limitations to this approach. As mentioned previously, we do not always have at our disposal clear, formal rules for determining priorities when faced with competing moral claims. In such situations we must go beyond casuistry and employ considerable analysis, critical reflection, and intuitive reasoning to determine which of the competing *prima facie* obligations possesses greater weight.[29] It is precisely because the Jewish moral system is pluralistic and operates with a variety of norms and values, which cannot simply be deduced from or justified by a single principle, that we must always examine the specific features of a given existential situation before informed ethical judgments can be made as to which of the conflicting norms overrides the other.[30]

II

Jewish tradition's emphasis upon casuistry, the recognition of the contextual setting of ethical principles, and the reliance upon ethical intuitions represent the very antithesis of the Kantian approach, which, because of its preoccupation with universalizability, dismisses the particular circumstances of a given situation as ethically irrelevant.[31] For Kant, morality was categorical; historic factors and contingencies had no bearing upon it. All that mattered was conformity to abstract formal principles. Thus, for example, he went so far as to condemn telling a lie even to save a human life.[32] Jewish morality, on the other hand, takes seriously the moral requirements arising from the particular features of a given historical situation, be they filial duties, obligations to benefactors, members of one's own family, community, or people. While some Christian moralists may contend that "Love thy neighbor as thyself" implies that, ideally, in matters involving concern for others, one should not discriminate between members of one's family and total strangers, since they are all equally entitled to our love, Jewish morality does not accept this basic premise. It does not espouse the kind of ethics that was ridiculed by Nietzsche as *Fernstenliebe* (love of the distant). Jewish Covenantal Ethics does not mandate that we love everyone equally. It is, instead, our duty to show every individual the kind of love that is appropriate to the relationship.

In contradistinction to Christianity, Jewish ethics does not create a dichotomy between self-seeking *eros* and self-surrendering *agape*. On the contrary, it recognizes the legitimacy of natural sentiments of self-love as well as the special bonds of closeness and concern for our own kin. Far from calling for the suppression of these healthy, natural sentiments, it mandates that we build upon them and draw into the orbit of our loving concern even those for whom we do not possess feelings of special closeness. As Nachmanides points out,[33] our own personal needs must be accorded priority, because "Thou shalt love thy neighbor as thyself" must be interpreted in such a manner that it does not conflict with the imperative "Thine own life takes precedence over that of others."[34] Similarly, members of one's own family are entitled to preferential treatment in the distribution of charity.[35] The prophet Isaiah expressed this idea most forcefully in his plea, "Thou shalt not hide thyself from thine own flesh."[36] By the same token, according to Jewish law, members of our own community have a greater claim on our resources than do outsiders. In the formulation of the Talmud, "the poor of your own city take precedence over the poor of another city."[37] Accordingly, we cannot establish priorities in allocating charitable funds simply by computing the maximal utility to mankind. A thousand dollars sent to Ethiopian famine relief would probably yield more benefit than the same amount spent to enhance the education of one's own child.[38] But parents must balance the concern for the good of humanity against the particular obligations incurred by them through having brought their child into the world.

Because historical factors enter into the determination of ethical requirements, a variety of specific moral obligations arise from such historical contingencies as having made promises or having been the recipient of benefactions. Gratitude ranks as one of the foremost religious values. Bahya Ibn Pakuda goes so far as to maintain that without a sense of gratitude it is impossible to be genuinely religious.[39] The Torah (Deut. 32:6) castigates Israel primarily for its ingratitude in forgetting that God is "thy Father that owns thee." Similarly, Israel's disloyalty is summed up in the charge, "Of the Rock that begot thee thou wast unmindful and didst forget God that bore thee."[40]

Gratitude dictates that parents, to whom we owe our very existence, be treated with honor and reverence. According to Rabbinic interpretation, the fifth commandment of the Decalogue includes the obligation to care for the physical, emotional, and financial needs of parents.[41] There is an irreducible debt of gratitude every one owes to a parent for being the source of one's very existence. In addition, Jewish children are indebted to their parents for conferring upon them the privilege of membership in the Covenantal community, through which their transcendent value system is mediated.

Among the fundamental requirements of filial piety are rendering services such as feeding, dressing, or taking a parent for a walk whenever such assistance is needed. Performance of even menial services should be viewed as a privilege—the opportunity to honor one's parents. Sometimes, however, the obligation to provide services to parents is a *prima facie* duty that may clash with other *prima facie* duties, especially those conflicting with obligations toward spouses or children. In such situations, obligations to parents must be viewed within the context of our total ethical responsibilities. There are no simple rules determining which of the competing *prima facie* obligations possesses the characteristic of overridingness. In many instances, the determination can be made only within the existential situation itself.[42]

III

Because Jewish morality takes seriously the particularities arising from historical contingencies and responds to the demands of communitarian considerations, there is no justification for Hermann Cohen's contention that aspirations for Jewish statehood have to be renounced on the ground that it is impossible for any state to conform to the rigorous standards demanded by his utopian Messianic ethics. Cohen's ethical system develops the Kantian doctrine of universalizability into a Messianic ethics, revolving around the ultimate ideal — the unity of mankind. Since a state is bound to give preference to its own interests over the claims of others, it is impossible to reconcile concern for a particular state with radical obedience to a universalistic ethics. This is one of the major reasons why Cohen was so unalterably opposed to modern Zionism. Obviously, had Cohen recognized that Jewish ethics, unlike Kant's, combines recognition of universal principles with sensitivity to particularistic concerns, he would have realized that ethical propriety is not solely determined by abstract general principles but also involves responsiveness to the specific requirements of historical communities. For that matter, had he been more attuned to the requirements of historical situations, he would not have insisted that we apply to our own unredeemed world standards suitable for a utopian Messianic society redeemed from all evil and oppression.[43]

Like Hermann Cohen, Ahad Ha'am completely ignored fundamental components of Jewish ethics, especially its sensitivity to factors arising from historical contingencies. He claimed, pointing to Hillel's negative formulation of the Golden Rule as justification, that Jewish ethics was a purely formal system totally preoccupied with abstract justice, to the exclusion of all other factors or values.[44] This, however, was a gross distortion of Jewish ethics. To begin with, Jewish ethics does not divorce the concern for justice completely from all utilitarian considerations. One can plausibly argue that Judaism accords a high priority to justice for reasons that resemble the approach of John Stuart Mill. One can refer to the practical utility of the rules of justice as necessary to the survival of society. One might further argue that the Torah links the pursuit of justice with the viability of a Jewish society in the Land of Israel. In the words of Deuteronomy,

> Justice, justice shall you pursue, that you may live and occupy the land that the Lord is giving you.[45]

To be sure, nothing in classical Jewish teachings is incompatible with the proposition that justice is an independent and intrinsic value that ought to be pursued for its own sake rather than its social utility. After all, the Torah surrounds the pursuit of justice with a special transcendent significance, declaring that "judgment is God's."[46] The Midrash goes so far as to declare that when a just verdict is obtained, there are no losers but only winners. The successful litigant obtains what is rightfully his, while the unsuccessful party gains by being relieved from the onus of claiming or holding illegitimate property.[47] In a similar vein, Ibn Ezra explains that the reason for the repetition of the word "justice" in the above-quoted admonition is that the litigant's primary objective should not be monetary gain, but—win or lose—the upholding of justice. It was in this spirit that the late Justice Silberg declared that the real goal of the Jewish legal system is not simply to provide procedures through which conflicting claims can be settled without recourse to force, but rather to clarify the respective obligations of the contending parties. Since the Jewish legal system represents a quest for justice rather than, as in our own American adversarial jurisprudence, a system that seeks to protect the rights of the conflicting litigants, it is readily understandable why Jewish jurisprudence functioned without recourse to lawyers, who are charged with representing the interests of their respective clients.[48]

But while it cannot be gainsaid that justice is a basic religio-ethical value, it does not follow, as Ahad Ha'am claimed, that justice revolves only around purely formal rules. In many cases,

Jewish law permits considerations of equity, over and above the requirements of abstract justice, to affect the determination of legal rights. Moreover, even in cases where concern for equity does not enable a court to set aside the legal rights of a party, Jewish ethics demands that one should not take advantage of the limitations of the legal system. Thus, even when a court cannot enforce restitution, it still has the authority to advise the party of a moral obligation to compensate the person who suffered a loss. Jewish jurisprudence recognizes claims that, while they are not enforced by the court, still possess some legal validity. These claims rest upon conceptions such as "being obligated by the Law of Heaven," "to discharge one's obligation to God," "to act in the manner of the pious," "thou shalt walk in the ways of the good," and so on.

Ahad Ha'am bases his view that Judaism only recognizes formal justice and leaves no room for love[49] upon the classic formulation of Rabbi Akiva,[50] who insisted that preserving one's own life takes precedence over preserving another's. But here Ahad Ha'am misreads Rabbi Akiva's ruling. It was not at all based upon concern for formal justice, which allegedly mandated disregard of particular circumstances and frowned upon making distinctions between human lives. On the contrary, Rabbi Akiva maintained that we must distinguish between lives and that each individual must accord priority to the preservation of his or her own life.

It is precisely because Jewish ethics places such emphasis upon the particularities arising from historical contingencies that we must reject the ahistorical conception of justice that has been developed by John Rawls in his widely acclaimed *A Theory of Justice*. A purely abstract, formal conception of justice that does not reckon with historical factors runs counter to the entire thrust of Jewish ethics.[51] We have previously mentioned Vidal Yom Tov of Tolosa's explanation of the Rabbinic decree that in the sale of real estate preferential treatment be given to the owners of adjoining real estate. In his opinion, the need for the enactment of this decree arose from the contingencies of history that give rise to different socioeconomic and cultural realities.[52] Thus, the developments of the historical process occasionally require that we modify and expand our notions of justice.

To return to our discussion of Ahad Ha'am's thesis, there is no basis for his claim that altruistic sentiments have no place within the Jewish ethical system. As was mentioned previously, it is precisely the interplay of a multiplicity of ethical values and norms that accounts for the uniqueness of the Jewish doctrine, with its demand to balance love with justice, universalism with particularism, self-love with altruism, quietism with activism, self-assertion with humility, submissiveness with creativity, self-realization with self-surrender, individual needs with social needs, and so forth.

It must be pointed out that our emphasis upon the need to weigh the relevant factors of a given situation in ethical decision-making does not lead to a purely situational ethics. Judaism is based upon the recognition of the validity and binding authority of general principles and laws. As we noted previously, unless a clear-cut legal norm of the Halakhah conflicts with other explicit halakhic prescriptions, it must be unconditionally obeyed. While we agree with Buber on the importance of making ethical decisions by focusing on the concrete, existential situation in the attempt to ascertain what are God's commands for us here and now, we unequivocally reject his antinomian position. For us, the Law is not a barrier between God and man, but a bridge to Him. Since Halakhah represents the Will of God, its rules and norms must reign supreme as our normative authority, unless superseded by other, more general halakhic principles. It is only when formal Halakhah is ambiguous or silent with respect to the demands of a given situation that our moral intuitions must bear the burden of ethical decision-making.

IV

It should not be surprising that the ethical domain confronts us with so many situations fraught with ambiguity. The Maimonidean doctrine of the "middle road" is a poignant reminder that ethics must balance various conflicting values. Rabbi Soloveitchik has pointed out that, for Maimonides, the advocacy of the middle road, in contrast with the Aristotelian notion, does not represent an ethics of compromise geared to the requirements of the successful man of affairs. Instead, it reflects an ethics of *imitatio dei.* "The middle road in which we are to walk . . . is the way of God."[53] Rabbi Soloveitchik interprets the Maimonidean conception with ideas derived from kabbalistic categories. According to the Kabbalah, it was the interplay of polar principles, such as love and justice, activity and passivity, expansion and contraction, that made possible the creation of the universe. Similarly, it is the mission of human beings to respond to the dialectical tension between polar values and to synthesize them in the attempt to lead a life of creativity.[54]

The challenge of accommodating conflicting principles and values is even more pronounced when we deal with ethical ideals rather than outright moral obligations. To begin with, the Jewish tradition operates with both activist and quietistic strands. It is largely a matter of personal predilections that determine which of these strands dominates our attitudes. Both derive from basic premises of Jewish metaphysics. On the one hand, Judaism stresses divine omnipotence. It cannot brook any limitations upon divine power. In the words of the liturgy, "Heal us, oh God, and we shall be healed, save us and we shall be saved."[55] The belief in divine omnipotence devalues human efforts and suggests that we are totally dependent upon God. But, on the other hand, human beings, as bearers of the divine image, must not be reduced to helpless puppets in the hands of an omnipotent deity. God is not only a saving God Who totally controls our destiny and Whose designs cannot be thwarted, but also a commanding God Who has willed that free acts of human beings are needed for the realization of some of His purposes. He has charged us to become His "partners in the process of creation."[56]

The Jewish faith experience, with its emphasis upon the centrality of the mitzvah, would not be possible without the belief that God demands human beings' *freely* given service, which, in turn, endows human existence with transcendent relevance. The more one contributes to the fulfillment of this divine task, the more meaning and value there are to one's existence. As the Mishnah expressed it, "Because the Holy One, blessed be He, wanted to confer special privileges upon Israel, he bestowed upon them such an abundance of Torah teachings and Commandments."[57]

Human freedom, creativity, and responsibility are indispensable to the fulfillment of the divinely assigned task, which involves more than blind submission to the divine will. For all its emphasis upon Revelation, Judaism rejects Tertullian's condemnation of reason and refuses to treat belief in the absurd as the hallmark of religion. In order to grasp the meaning of the divinely revealed Torah, human beings must exercise their rational faculties and employ their moral intuitions. "Torah is not in Heaven."[58] The traditional conception of the Oral Torah includes the belief that the meaning of the Torah can only be ascertained through a process of interaction between a finite human mind and data obtained through supernatural Revelation. Hence, human beings function together with God as active partners in creating the Torah.[59]

Reflecting the polar tension between divine omnipotence and human responsibility, we encounter within the Jewish tradition a wide range of attitudes toward human efforts to improve our own living conditions. Ibn Ezra, the medieval Bible exegete, disparaged all human efforts to enhance our material well-being. There is no point, he argued, in seeking to ameliorate one's lot, if human beings' material conditions are exclusively determined by divine Providence.[60] In a similar vein, Bahya Ibn Pakuda censured individuals who undertake arduous business trips. Could not the Almighty provide for the needs of the businessman if he stayed at home?[61]

Many traditional Jewish thinkers exhibit considerable sympathy for such pietism and quietism and admonish believers to leave some things to God. Yet Judaism, contrary to the distortions of it in the writings of Spinoza, Feuerbach, and Marx, does not engender the kind of self-alienation that strips human beings of all dignity. There is really no basis within Judaism for the canard that the advocacy of humility and the concomitant condemnation of the sin of pride on the part of religion inhibit human efforts and give rise to an abject sense of dependence that breeds passivity. That humility has nothing to do with the kind of quietism that stifles human initiative can be demonstrated by the fact that Moses, who is regarded as the very model of vigorous leadership, is extolled in the Torah for his extraordinary humility.[62] His utter self-effacement did not interfere with his ability to exercise dynamic leadership, because his historic achievements were inspired by the selfless quest to realize God's purposes and objectives, not by personal ambition or the desire for self-aggrandizement.

Contrary to Nietzsche's claim, humility is a sign of strength rather than of weakness. The Talmud notes that whenever the Torah refers to the might of God, His humility is also stressed.[63] Adopting the Lurianic metaphysical doctrine of *Tzimtzum* (divine self-contraction), Rabbi Soloveitchik explains this talmudic statement on the basis of the kabbalistic conception that divine Creation was possible only because God's humility manifested itself in His willingness to make room for beings other than Himself.[64]

As an attribute of an omnipotent Creator, humility can hardly be associated with fatalistic acquiescence to the status quo. Genuine humility, far from inhibiting, can actually inspire relentless efforts to fulfill our mission of perfecting the process of Creation in partnership with the divine Creator. Ideally, all human efforts, including those aiming at the preservation of one's physical and psychological well-being, should reflect the spirit of humility and should be regarded as the means not to self-centered ends, but to the fulfillment of our religious task.

According to the Talmud, "Let all your deeds be performed for the sake of Heaven" constitutes an all-inclusive formulation of the range of Jewish piety.[65] The ideal of humility as defined in terms of totally selfless service to God was expanded by Rabbi Chaim of Volozin to encompass prayer as well as action. For those who have reached the highest rungs of piety, prayer is no longer concerned with obtaining personal benefits, but is motivated by the supplicant's desire to reduce the suffering that God endures when one of His creatures is afflicted. Thus, even when praying for recovery from illness, our objective should not be to reduce our own suffering but to diminish the anguish experienced by the *Shekhinah* (Divine Presence) for our suffering.[66]

This emphasis upon humility by no means detracts from an individual's ontological worth. Significantly, even advocates of pietism and quietism attribute enormous significance to some forms of human activity — for example, the performance of *mitzvot*. In the kabbalistic scheme, human actions have repercussions not only in this world, but affect the highest regions of being and God's relationship to the world. This type of mysticism does not seek the dissolution of the self through mystic union with God;[67] for once the self is lost completely, becoming absorbed in the divine reality, it is no longer capable of responding to its mandated task. A Covenantal relationship is possible only when the human self retains its individuality and distinctiveness.

"The Torah was not given to angels,"[68] so the Rabbis affirm, but to human beings. Judaism does not seek the experience of being "turned on" by a higher reality, encountered in a mystical state of consciousness where all spatial and temporal distinctions are transcended. It aims at the fulfillment of God's will in the here-and-now. In the Jewish scale of values,

> Extending hospitality to strangers is of greater significance than encountering the *Shekhinah*.[69]

Significantly, in *Targum Onkelos,* the Aramaic translation of the Torah, the passage "the people come to me to seek God"[70] is rendered "the people come to me to seek instruction from God." In other words, seeking God primarily manifests itself in living in accordance with the Will of God.

This approach stands in marked contrast to that of Hellenistic religions. They advocated escape from the limitations of our existential world by flights into higher spiritual realms of being. Their ideal was the attainment of ecstasy, a state of consciousness that was supposed to liberate human beings from the confines of the physical world and enable them to apprehend transcendent realms. As the word "enthusiasm," literally "being in God," suggests, Hellenistic cults maintained that it was possible for human beings to participate in the divine. Since for Hellenism the universe was a necessary emanation of divinity, there was no radical discontinuity between God and the world.[71]

In Judaism an unbridgeable chasm separates God and human beings. God is the Creator, Whose being is utterly incommensurable with that of His creatures. This doctrine rules out both the divinization of man and the naturalization of God. In the words of Exodus, "Man cannot see Me and live."[72] Piety expresses itself in the attempt to respond to God by obedience to His revealed will. The very finitude of human existence represents not metaphysical evil but the source of a person's ontological worth. The human task is to act in the spatio-temporal world in accordance with divine norms that link us to the transcendental realm. As Rabbi Soloveitchik articulated so eloquently, even when an individual has attained the supernatural gift of prophecy and has beheld the heavenly mysteries, the prophet eventually must return to this- worldly responsibilities as the bearer of a socio-ethical message.[73]

V

Because so much emphasis is placed upon human responsibility to God for this-worldly actions, no echoes of the Promethean myth are heard in Judaism. Totally absent is any suggestion that the exercise of human creativity in the development of science or technology represents an unwarranted intrusion into divine prerogatives.

There is, however, no unanimity concerning the type of creativity that is not merely condoned but mandated. In the opinion of Rabbi Chaim of Volozin,[74] for example, only creativity directed toward the spiritual realm possesses religious significance. Solely through the quest for spiritual perfection can human beings fulfill their role in the universe. In keeping with this pietistic stance, all efforts to improve the socio-political conditions of the world, and especially of the Jewish people, are exercises in futility. For *galut* (the Exile) and the various forms of

physical suffering of the Jewish people are merely epipheno-
mena of the real malaise — the state of spiritual fallenness. As the
Jewish liturgy proclaims, "Because of our sins, we were expelled
from our land."[75] According to this view, the sins of the Jewish
people were responsible for the destruction of the Temple. The
Babylonians or the Romans merely functioned as the instru-
ments of divine retribution. Hence, the Redemption can only be
brought about through thorough-going spiritual regeneration
effectuated by intensive Torah study and meticulous observance
of the divine Law.[76]

In the formulation of his own religious philosophy, R. Joseph
B. Soloveitchik, a descendant of R. Chaim of Volozin, interprets
the same biblical and Rabbinic material to reach completely
different conclusions. To him, the Bible not only allows but actually mandates that man subdue nature and harness its forces
to his purposes. When human beings engage in the conquest of
nature to enhance human welfare, they are not guilty of hubris
or of usurping powers rightfully belonging to God, but they are
carrying out a God-given mission.

Similarly, the Rabbinic interpretation of the story of the
Tower of Babel makes no reference to one of the central elements of Greek mythology, the belief that humanity's success in
the conquest of nature arouses the jealousy of the deity. In Judaism, what provoked the divine wrath was not humanity's technological triumph but their idolatry — their arrogant proclama-
tion of human independence from God, leading to the worship
of the collectivity.

But it is one thing to condemn defiance of God's supremacy,
and another to maintain that our intellectual, cultural, and technological attainments inevitably implicate us in guilt. Judaism
contends that we can affirm human dignity without plunging
into an abyss of self-idolization. To be human entails the steer-
ing of a middle course between self-deification and self-
degradation. We must neither play God nor sink to the level of
animals. Since, according to the Psalmist, man is made "but little
lower than the angels . . . and to have dominion over the works
of Thy hands,"[77] Judaism cannot subscribe to William James's

thesis that "the abandonment of self-responsibility" is the hall-mark of the religious attitude.

Scientific and technological triumphs become objectionable when they engender arrogance, which manifests itself in the tendency to pursue science as an end in itself, with utter disregard for their human or ecological cost. We witness this lack of humility when scientists fail to ascertain, before embarking upon genetic engineering or other technological projects, whether the projected benefits will outweigh potential genetic or ecological damage. The earth is not ours. We are responsible to God for the preservation of His world. When conquest of nature for the enhancement of human welfare is viewed not as an act of self-assertion but as a religious obligation, conservation of non-replenishable resources and protection of the environment cease to be mere matters of prudence but acquire the status of ethico-religious imperatives.

Since the hazards of technological progress were recognized only recently, it can hardly be expected that classical Jewish sources would offer any specific recommendation on how to balance concern for the material welfare of our contemporaries with our responsibilities for the future. We can, however, extrapolate from halakhic data general guidelines, emphasizing our responsibility to take account not only of immediate economic benefits but also to concern ourselves with the impact of our policies upon generations to come.

The Jewish tradition reflects the tension between divine omnipotence and human freedom, between reliance upon the divine providential design and the exercise of human responsibility.[78] It should hardly come as a surprise that in the wake of the Emancipation and the Enlightenment, thinkers such as Samson R. Hirsch, Rav Kook, and Rav Joseph B. Soloveitchik, who displayed openness to the values of modernity, tended to stress human responsibility,[79] while those who looked askance at these revolutionary transformations and preferred the protective walls of the ghetto were prone to disparage involvement in science and technology. It was natural for the more traditionally inclined circles to gravitate toward quietistic attitudes, because, ever since the debacle of the Bar Kokhba rebellion, conditions dictated the adoption of a completely submissive and fatalistic stance, with no attempt to regain national independence. This approach is most pronounced among the Neturei Karta, who condemn the Zionist revolution not merely because it espoused a secular nationalism, but because, in their opinion, all human efforts to achieve national liberation reflect a lack of faith in God, Who alone can dispense salvation through a supernatural Messiah.

This orientation also leads to the rejection of various forms of sociopolitical activism. Segments of the traditional community have frowned upon efforts to secure Jewish political rights on the ground that if God really wanted the amelioration of the abject conditions of the Jewish people, He could bring this about without requiring the assistance of Jewish political action. The historical record shows that Hungarian Orthodoxy, for example, was unequivocally opposed to any interventions with governmental authorities designed to improve the sociopolitical or economic conditions of the Jewish community. That this quietistic stance was not only prompted by the fear that better socioeconomic and political realities would expose the Jewish community to the spiritual hazards of assimilation, but also reflected a deeply ingrained and genuine aversion to any form of activism, can be gauged by a remarkable comment of R. Abraham Samuel Benjamin Sofer, the son and successor of the Hatam Sofer. He notes that Noah is first described in Genesis (6:9) as a perfectly righteous individual, whereas subsequently (Gen. 7:1) he is characterized merely as a righteous individual but not as a perfect one. R. Sofer suggests that this diminution of Noah's status occurred because, according to the Midrash, Noah's invention of the plow paved the way for the development of agriculture. With the improved ability to grow food, people no longer felt completely dependent upon God. Thus, Noah contributed to the process of secularization.[80]

Some pietists even discourage recourse to any form of medical intervention, despite the fact that it is explicitly licensed by Halakhah. Indeed, most halakhic authorities regard resorting to medical help as an outright religious obligation. But there are others who view any reliance upon medical procedures as a sign of lack of faith in God. As Nachmanides put it, "the person of genuine faith will have no need for physicians.[81]

It is thus apparent that Halakhah permits a wide range of attitudes toward the religious legitimacy or desirability of sociopolitical activism. My view is in complete disagreement with that of Professor Scholem, who claimed that believers in the ultimate Messianic Redemption cannot attach real significance to actions performed by unredeemed individuals.[82] In his opinion, it is a corollary of the Messianic idea that the ultimate Redemption can only be brought about by overt divine intervention. Hence, natural processes cannot contribute to the realization of the ultimate goal of history and, therefore, are essentially meaningless. But this line of reasoning is faulty. One could easily turn the argument around and contend that the assurance of God's ultimate intervention in the historical process guarantees that human efforts to establish justice and benevolence are not senseless gestures but stepping stones toward the realization of the ideals that will ultimately triumph in the Kingdom of God.[83]

Conclusion

I N THE PRECEDING CHAPTER I CALLED ATTENTION to some of the perplexing issues encountered in environmental ethics, in allocating scarce resources to health care, in the balancing of concern for the sanctity versus the quality of life, in the withholding of unfavorable information, and the like. Our discussion reveals that, especially when faced with novel conditions, Jewish Covenantal Ethics, for all its commitment to absolute norms, does not have ready-made answers to all questions. We also observed, as we previously noted in chapters 2 and 5, that many ethical issues leave us no alternative but to rely upon intuitive ethical judgments for their resolution.

But it is one thing to admit that we do not know the answers, and another to claim that there are no answers. For all its vagueness in matters that are not covered by halakhic legislation, Jewish Covenantal Ethics reflects the conviction that statements about right and wrong, good and evil, are not just matters of arbitrary convention or reflections of culturally determined, relativistic value judgments. Despite the fact that they are not empirically verifiable, they are objectively either true or false. Moreover, to the extent that many ethical judgments (such as prohibitions against theft, murder, or torture) are explicitly formulated in what are acknowledged as divinely revealed norms, they must, for all their pluralism, be mutually compatible with each other. As I have shown in chapter 6, it is inconceivable that a divine system of norms is self-contradictory.

Secular pluralistic systems of ethics, on the other hand, can provide no assurance that their basic premises will not eventually lead to self-contradictory conclusions. As the famous mathematician Goedel has demonstrated in his revolutionary theorem, it is impossible to prove the consistency of any deductive system. Only when the various constituent parts of a pluralistic ethical system are attributed to a divine source (communicated either through supernatural Divine Revelation or, as for Jewish rationalists, through reason) does it become possible to remove all doubts concerning the tenability, feasibility, and consistency of a pluralistic ethical system.

This emphasis upon the objective validity of ethical judgments is perfectly compatible with maintaining that what is right or wrong at a given time may also be influenced by contingent historical factors. After all, Jewish ethics, in large measure, addresses itself to the regulation of conduct. Only followers of Kant can disregard all empirical data and argue that ethics revolves exclusively around eternally valid truths of reason, because in their view ethics is concerned only with intentions and is completely indifferent to the actual consequences of actions. As was pointed out in chapter 1 in connection with the explanation of the rule granting the right of pre-emption to owners of adjoining land, historical developments may exert a profound influence upon what kind of conduct is morally desirable. Thus, for example, the standards of sexual morality acceptable in a polygamous civilization would hardly be suitable to a monogamous society. Similarly, a patriarchal society would naturally view filial obligations or the status of women in a different light from what would be considered proper under contemporary circumstances. Moreover, new scientific findings, as those, for example, about the effects of technology upon the environment, are bound to affect perceptions of what constitutes ethically appropriate behavior.

Jewish law does not always keep pace with the latest advances in ethical thought. While legal systems generally gravitate toward conservatism, the lack of a universally recognized halakhic authority makes Halakhah even more resistant to change than other legal systems. Even the ban against polygamy was accepted only by Western but not by Oriental Jewish communities. In recent years, the time lag between the emergence of moral beliefs and their formal incorporation into the halakhic system has grown considerably, because many rabbis harbor increasing doubts about their own authority and hesitate to issue novel decrees. This accounts for the reluctance of most rabbinic authorities to endorse an outright halakhic prohibition against smoking, despite the fact that smoking is widely perceived as a serious health hazard.

Because of its proclivity for conservatism, the formal Halakhah may not always keep abreast of the rapid pace of modern developments, but Jewish Covenantal Ethics, as noted in chapter 2, may fill the gap by *recommending* conduct that goes beyond legal requirements in reflecting sensitivity to ethical concerns. It should be borne in mind that it is only in the area of ethics and not within the domain of ritual law that Judaism mandates going beyond minimal legal requirements. As noted in chapter 5, Maimonides' special attention to the ethical sphere is closely linked to his advocacy of virtue-ethics, which treats the cultivation of an ethical disposition as an outright religious obligation. But even those who do not share this perspective recognize that the ethical sphere contains unique and distinctive features that differentiate it from purely ritual laws.

That, however, is a far cry from treating religion simply as a postulate of ethics. Even such an ardent Kantian as Hermann Cohen realized in his later development that religion cannot be dissolved into ethics,[1] because faith in the God of Israel includes elements that transcend the realm of the ethical. Religion is not a handmaiden of ethics. On the contrary, ethical conduct, especially to the extent that it involves imitation of the ways of God, is an avenue to Him.[2] The widely copied practice of R. Eleazar, who gave charity *before* the recital of prayers, illustrates this point.[3] He did not treat prayer as a prelude to ethical living. Instead, basing his practice on the biblical verse, "I shall behold Thy face with righteousness" (Ps. 17:15), he looked upon ethical conduct as a prerequisite for proper communion with God.

Classical Jewish texts, especially in Leviticus, employ the term "holiness" in a manner that cannot be reconciled with the Kantian doctrine that holiness is a purely ethical category. The Jewish conception points to a realm of what Rudolf Otto described as the realm of the "wholly other." Because Jewish ethics is, in the final analysis, grounded in the religious imperative of imitating the ways of God rather than merely in prudential considerations of social utility, it is not surprising that, as observed in chapter 4, it includes unique features that distinguish it from secular ethics systems.

Ethics is prescriptive rather than descriptive. It deals with the "ought," not with the "is." Unlike the laws of nature, which presuppose complete causal determination, ethics is possible only, as Kant has shown, when the actions of rational agents are not exclusively determined by causal factors. But this does not imply that ethics should be oblivious to realities and human limitations and advocate "impossible ideals."

Although the Messianic hope figures very prominently in Jewish thought, it simply does not make sense to be guided in our unredeemed world by principles that would be appropriate if all evil were overcome and human beings acted in accordance with the requirements of a rational morality. What we ought to do in the here-and-now cannot be based upon what we ought to do under ideal conditions; it must be predicated, rather, upon our prudential assessment of the realities of human nature.

A Jewish ethics that reflects halakhic categories must be geared to the requirements of real people in the real world. "The Torah was not given to angels."[4] Moreover, "the Torah addresses the evil urge."[5] For all its aversion to violence, Jewish ethics, as shown in chapter 5, rejects pacifism and mandates resistance to evil. The real world cannot be governed by utopian ethical principles.

The same realism necessitates the distinction between obligatory and supererogatory conduct. Hermann Cohen contended that a religious ethics can make no such distinction. It was for this reason that he dismissed Maimonides' espousal of an ethics of the middle road as a mere "survival" of a secular Aristotelian ethics. We have seen that the ideal of supererogatory conduct must be distinguished from the notion of an outright moral obligation. In contrast to completely objective moral obligations, ethical ideals are more subjective because they must take account of the actual potential of the individuals involved. As Maimonides expressed it with respect to the imitation of the divine moral attributes, ideals must be geared to the requirements of the different "capacities of each individual."

This doctrine can be developed beyond what Maimonides would have been prepared to accept. It can serve as a point of departure for a pluralistic ethics that admits a variety of visions of the good. To be sure, Maimonides shares the view of Aristotle and of many classical thinkers who maintain that there is only one proper conception of the ideal way of life. But from a purely Jewish point of view, it is quite possible to contend, as we did in chapter 6, that, as long as their conduct conforms to halakhic standards, individuals are free to select whatever ideals are most suitable to their respective personalities. Since each individual bears the image of God in a unique way, it is to be expected that there are many diverse ways in which we may best develop our potential for spiritual fulfillment.

Notes

INTRODUCTION

1. Deut. 28:9.
2. See Emil Brunner, *The Divine Imperative*, trans. Olive Wyon (Philadelphia: Westminster Press, 1936); Paul Lehmann, *Ethics in a Christian Context* (New York: Harper and Row, 1963); H. Richard Niehbur, *The Responsible Self* (New York: Harper and Row, 1963); Erich Fromm, *You Shall Be as Gods* (New York: Holt, Rinehart and Winston, 1966).
3. See my "Meta-Halakhic Propositions," in *Leo Jung Jubilee Volume*, ed. Menahem M. Kasher, Norman Lamm, and Leonard Rosenfeld (New York: Jewish Center, 1962), 211–221; *idem*, "Covenantal Imperatives," in *Samuel K. Mirsky Memorial Volume*, ed. Gersion Appel (New York: Yeshiva University, 1970) 3–12; *idem*, "Law as the Basis of a Moral Society," *Tradition* 19, 1 (1981): 42–54; *idem*, "Foundations of Jewish Ethics," in *The Solomon Goldman Lectures* (Chicago: Spertus College of Judaica Press, 1990), 5:119–129.
4. *Sefer Chazon Ish*, ed. S. Greineman (Jerusalem: Hamasorah, 1954), 21–43; Isaiah Leibowitz, *Torah U'Mitzvot Bazeman hazeh* (Tel Aviv: Massadah Press, 1954); Marvin Fox, "Reflections on the Foundations of Jewish Ethics and Their Relation to Public Policy," in *The Society of Christian Ethics, 1980 Selected Papers*, ed. Joseph L. Allen (Dallas, 1980), 21–63; *idem, Interpreting Maimonides* (Chicago: University of Chicago Press, 1990), 199–226. Cf. also David Bleich, "Is There an Ethics Beyond Halakhah?" in *Proceedings of the Ninth World Congress of Jewish Studies* (Jerusalem: World Congress of Jewish Studies, 1985), 55–62.

My own position is much closer to that of Aharon Lichtenstein's "Does Jewish Tradition Recognize an Ethics of Halakhah?" in *Modern Jewish Ethics*, ed. Marvin Fox (Columbus: Ohio State University Press, 1975), 60–88, and to that of Shubert Spero, *Halakhah, Morality and the Jewish Tradition*, ed. Norman Lamm, The Library of Jewish Law and Ethics, vol. 9 (New York and Hoboken: Ktav and Yeshiva University Press, 1983), 21–63.

5. Nachmanides, Torah Commentary to Deut. 6:18.

6. Cf. Robert Gordis, *Judaism For the Modern Age* (New York: Farrar, Strauss, 1955); *idem, The Dynamics of Judaism* (Bloomington: Indiana University Press, 1990); Emil L. Fackenheim, *Quest for Past and Future* (Bloomington: Indiana University Press, 1968), 66–82, 96–111; *idem, What is Judaism?* (New York: Summit Books, 1987), 98–102; Eugene Borowitz, *Renewing the Covenant* (Philadelphia: The Jewish Publication Society, 1991); *idem, Exploring the Covenant* (Detroit: Wayne State University Press, 1990), 163–225; Herman E. Schaalman, "Revelation, a Prologomenon," in *Through the Sound of Many Voices,* ed. Jonathan E. Plaut (Toronto: Lester and Orpen Dennys, 1982), 81–93; Louis Jacobs, *A Jewish Theology* (New York: Behrman House, 1973), 199–230.

7. This verse (Deut. 30:12) is quoted in B. Bava Metzia 59b as prooftext that Torah should be interpreted in accordance with standard hermeneutical principles rather than by reliance on "heavenly voices" or other supernatural modes of communication.

8. Bernard Williams, *Ethics and the Limits of Philosophy* (Cambridge, Mass.: Harvard University Press, 1985).

CHAPTER ONE

1. For a comprehensive treatment of the subject, see Spero, *Halakhah,* 21–63.

2. Gen. 18:19.

3. Exod. 15:25. See, especially, Nachmanides, Torah Commentary *ad. loc.* Cf. also Maimonides, *Guide,* Part III, 32.

4. The "latter prophets": Isa. 1:11–17, 5:16; Jer. 9:23; Amos 5:21–24; Mic. 6:8.

5. J. Nedarim 9:4.

6. B. Berakhot 47b; Sukkah 30a.

7. B. Bava Kamma 94a; Sanhedrin 6b.

8. B. Yoma 88b.

9. B. Sanhedrin 74a.

10. Ibid.

11. B. Berakhot 43b; Sotah 10b. R. Ovadia Yoseph, in his *Yabia Omer,* vol. 6, 187–188, considers this talmudic statement not merely as an Aggadic hyperbole but as an outright religious imperative. See S. A. Abraham, "Pikuach Nefesh U'Mitzvot Shebein Adam Lechavero," *Ha'Ma'ayan* 20, 2 (Tevet, 5740): 22–23.

12. B. Bava Kamma 60b.

13. See Chaim Chizkeyahu Medini, *Sedei Chemed Hashalem* (Benei Berak: Beit Hasofer), 1:16.

14. Abraham, "Pikuach Nefesh," 23–24.

15. Ps. 19:1 and 8.

16. B. Avodah Zarah 3a; Shabbat 33a.

17. For references, see Theodore Hiebert, "Ecology and the Bible," *Harvard Divinity Bulletin* (Fall 1989) 19:7.

18. Deut. 25:4. See also Maimonides, *Guide,* Part III, 48 and Ibn Ezra, Commentary to Deut. 22:10.

There are conflicting opinions in the Talmud whether inflicting any kind of unnecessary pain upon animals is prohibited by the Torah or whether it is merely Rabbinic ordinance. See B. Sabbath 128b; Bava Metzia 32b. For a discussion of this question, see Medini, *Sedei Chemed Hashalem,* 5:265.

19. Nachmanides, Torah Commentary, Deut. 22:6.

20. Deut. 20:19–20. The Rabbis extended the prohibition to encompass all un-necessary destruction of property and even to the wasting of materials. See *Encyclo-paedia Talmudit,* vol. 3, *s.v.* "Bal Tashchit."

21. Lev. 19:18.

22. Ibid. 19:2.

23. Ps. 24:1, 1 Chron. 29:11–14; Avot 3:7; B. Berakhot 6b.

24. For a brilliant analysis of the ethical implications of the doctrine that God is the Creator, see Hans Jonas, *Philosophical Essays: From Ancient Creed to Technological Man* (Chicago: Chicago University Press, 1974), 21–44, 168–182.

25. See Charles Taliaferro, "God's Estate," *The Journal of Religious Ethics* (Spring 1992), 20:69–92. Compare also Baruch A. Brody's essay, "Morality and Religion Reconsidered," in *Readings in the Philosophy of Religion* ed. Baruch A. Brody (Englewood Cliffs: Prentice Hall, 1974), 592–603.

26. Tosefta Berakhot 4:1.

27. Genesis Rabbah 100:1, in a comment on Ps. 100:3, notes that awareness of belonging to God prods us to strive for ever higher levels of moral and spiritual perfection.

28. See Introduction, n. 4.

29. See Wurzburger, "Jewish Ethics," 119.

30. Commentary to Mishnah, Avot 1:1. In striking contrast to this view, R. Judah Loew ben Bezalel, commenting on the same text in his *Derekh Ha'chaim,* emphasizes that the ethical views expressed in *Avot* were not derived from the Sinaitic Revelation but reflect valid ethical insights of eminent religious personalities.

31. This threefold classification of the Commandments is provided by Elijah Gaon in his Commentary to Prov. 2:9.

32. Joseph B. Soloveitchik, *Chamesh Derashot* (Jerusalem: Machon Tal Orot, 1974), 87–97.

Although some talmudic statements credit Abraham with the observance of all the commandments that were taught him by "his innards" long before the Sinaitic legislation, it must be realized that the only ritual observance mandated in the Covenant with Abraham was the practice of circumcision. See Arthur Green, *Devotion and Commandment* (Cincinnati: Hebrew Union College Press, 1989).

33. In Rabbi Soloveitchik's "Kol Dodi Dofek," in *Besod Hayachid Ve'hayachad* (Jerusalem: Machon Tal Orot, 1976), 362–377, the Covenant that, prior to the Exodus, provided the basis of the formation of the Jewish community as an involuntary Community of Fate is termed "The Covenant of Egypt" or alternately *Berit Rishonim,* "Covenant with the Ancestors."

34. Rabbi Soloveitchik expressed this view in a lecture entitled "The Religious Experience," which he delivered at the Convention of the Rabbinical Council of America, held at Ste. Agathe, Quebec, in 1960. Unfortunately, the text of this seminal and widely discussed lecture was never published.

35. Fromm, *Gods,* 56.

36. Rudolf Bultmann, *Jesus and the World* (New York: Charles Scribner's Sons, 1934), 69.

37. Prov. 3:6.

38. B. Berakhot 63a. See Wurzburger, "Moral Society," 51.

39. Avot 2:12. See also B. Beitzah 16a, which attributes this maxim to Hillel.

40. See G. E. Moore, *Principia Ethica* (Cambridge: Cambridge University Press, 1903).

41. See Jeffrey Stout, *Ethics After Babel* (Boston: Beacon Press, 1988), 109–123.

42. Lichtenstein, "Ethics of Halakhah," 60–88.

43. Moore, *Principia Ethica*.

44. *The Religion of Israel: From its Beginnings to the Babylonian Exile,* trans. and abr. Moshe Greenberg (New York: Schocken Books, 1972), 234.

45. Rav Nissim Gaon's Introduction to the Babylonian Talmud was published in the Shulsinger edition of the Babylonian Talmud (New York, 1948), 1:1.

46. Ibid. Historically, the first attempt to identify the Seven Laws of Noah with the "natural law" was made by Philo. See Harry Austryn Wolfson, *Philo: Foundations of Religious Philosophy in Judaism, Christianity and Islam* (Cambridge, Mass.: Harvard University Press, 1947), 2:180–187. Yitzchak F. Baer was mistaken when he asserted that it was in the writings of Isaac Abravanel that the identity of the natural law and the seven Noahide Laws was for the first time established; see Baer's *Galut* (New York: Schocken Books, 1947), 62. In his *Devotion and Commandment: The Faith of Abraham in the Hasidic Imagination* (Cincinnati: Hebrew Union College, 1989), 38, Arthur Green points out that David Kimchi contended that the Noahide Laws included also *chukim* (nonrational ritual commandments). On the other hand, a highly respected recent halakhic authority, R. Meir Simchah of Dvinsk, maintains in his *Meshekh Chakhmah* (commentary to Deut. 13:4) that the seven Noahide Commandments are rationally necessary and therefore universally applicable.

A useful discussion of Jewish attitudes toward natural law is found in Salo Wittmayer Baron, *A Social and Religious History of the Jews* (Philadelphia: Jewish Publication Society, 1958), 6:144–145. For biographical references, see p. 397, n. 167 in the same volume. See also David S. Shapiro, "Torat Ha-anashut al pi Mekorot Hayahadut," in *Orachim* (Jerusalem: Mossad Harav Kook, 1977), 33–54; Samuel Atlas, *Netivim Bamishpat Haivri* (New York: American Academy for Jewish Research, 1978), 1–40; and Aaron Lichtenstein, *The Seven Laws of Noah* (New York: Rabbi Jacob Joseph School Press, 1981), 5.

47. See Marvin Fox, "Maimonides and Aquinas on Natural Law," *Dinei Yisrael* III (1972): 5–36; Joseph Faur, *Iyunim Be-mishneh Torah: Sefer Hamada* (Jerusalem: Mossad Harav Kook, 1978). For the view that Maimonides operated with a natural law doctrine, see Atlas, *Netivim*, 1–40. I am especially impressed by Atlas's argument that Maimonides' peroration at the conclusion of *Hilkhot Shemittah Ve'yovel* shows that for a non-Jew the acknowledgment of the Mosaic authority of the moral law is not an indispensable requirement for the achievement of religious perfection (as opposed to obtaining the legal status of a *Ger Toshav*). See also the incisive discussions of the entire issue in David Novack, *The Image of the Non-Jew in Judaism* (New York: Edwin Mellen, 1983), and Isadore Twersky, *Introduction to the Code of Maimonides* (New Haven and London: Yale University Press, 1980), 456–458. Cf.

also *The Pursuit of the Ideal: Jewish Writings of Steven Schwarzschild,* ed. Menachem Kellner (Albany: State University of New York Press, 1990), 50–59 and, especially, 309–331.

Marvin Fox correctly pointed out in the above-cited paper that until Albo, the term "natural law" never appeared in Jewish philosophical literature. But failure to employ this particular term can hardly serve as evidence that there was no attempt to invoke the authority of reason, common sense, or conscience as justification of moral laws.

It is also noteworthy that contemporary halakhic authorities, without discussing the underlying philosophical issues, disagree with Professor Fox's stance and take it for granted that for Maimonides, moral and religious obligations need not necessarily derive from Revelation but may be grounded in rational perceptions. Significantly, Rabbi Yehudah Gershuni, in his *Kol Tzofayikh* (Brooklyn: Moriah, 1980), 129, contends that for Maimonides, the religious obligation to reside in the Land of Israel has no scriptural basis but constitutes a dictate of rationality. A far more plausible explanation for Maimonides' view that, in spite of the fact that there is no specific passage upon which such a requirement can be based, there is a religious obligation to settle in Israel, is offered by Nachum Rabinovitch in his essay, "Possession of the Land of Israel," in *Crossroads: Halacha and the Modern World* (Zomet: Alon Shevut, 1988), 2:203–205.

Another example of the attempt by contemporary Halakhists to base religious requirements exclusively upon purely ethical obligations is provided by Rabbi Chaim David Halevi, who in his essay, "Darkhei Shalom Beyachasim Shebein Hayehudim Lishe'einam Yehudim," in *Techumin* (Zomet: Alon Shevut, 1988), 9:71–81, argues that the obligation to render assistance to non-Jews (with the exception of those practicing idolatry) is an outright moral obligation, which requires no scriptural support whatsoever. (See chap. 3, n. 57 in this volume).

48. Abraham Yitzchak Hakohen Kook, *Orot Hakodesh* (Jerusalem: Mossad Harav Kook, 1964), 3:1–35.

49. See chap. 3.

50. Judah Loew ben Bezalel, "Netiv Derekh Eretz," in *Netivot Olam*, vol. 2.

51. *Aruch Ha-shulchan, Yoreh Deah* (240:2–3). In a similar vein, R. Shneur Zalman Mi-Ladi states, in his *Igeret Hakodesh* (chap. 12), that, ideally, the giving of charity should not be merely the expression of a naturally benevolent disposition but should be inspired by the religious ideal of total self-effacement, which calls for the subordination of one's own inclinations in the service of God. It should, however, be noted that in Maharal Mi-prag's opinion, a charitable act that is performed out of a sense of duty to comply with a divinely decreed ordinance but without any genuine desire to help a fellow human being does not qualify as having been fulfilled with the proper motivation required for this particular commandment (*Gur Aryeh, Sefer Shemot, s.v.* "U'velashon," p. 127). As noted later in the chapter on agent-morality, Judah Loew ben Bezalel's position is similar to that of Maimonides.

52. *Sefer ha-Ikkarim*, Part 3.

53. Avot 2:12. Maimonides, M. T. Hilkhot De'ot, 3:12. Cf. also Commentary to Mishneh, "Eight Chapters," chap. 5.

54. See Wurzburger, "Jewish Ethics," 121.

55. Cf. also the thorough critique of the Kantian position on the *Akedah* in Emil

L. Fackenheim, *Encounters Between Judaism and Modern Philosophy: A Preface to Future Jewish Thought* (New York: Basic Books, 1973), 33–37.

56. R. M. Hare, *Moral Thinking* (Oxford: Clarendon Press, 1981), 25–26.

57. See Nathan Rotenstreich, *Jewish Philosophy in Modern Times,* (New York: Holt, Rinehart and Winston, 1968), 4–10.

58. Michael Wyschogrod, *The Body of Faith* (Minneapolis: Seabury Press, 1983), chap. 5.

59. See Williams, *Ethics.*

60. M. T., Avadim 9:8.

61. G. E. M. Anscombe, "Modern Moral Philosophy," *Journal of Philosophical Studies* 33, (1958), 13–14.

62. H. A. Prichard, "Does Moral Philosphy Rest Upon a Mistake?" *Mind,* N.S. 4, (1912), 20–37.

63. Martin Buber, *At the Turning: Three Addresses on Judaism* (New York: Farrar, Straus and Young, 1952), 56; *Between Man and Man,* trans. Ronald Gregor Smith (New York: MacMillan Company, 1948), 16, 45.

64. See Wurzburger, "Moral Society," 42–52. Much of this chapter's discussion of the overridingness of moral imperatives is based upon this article.

65. See Wurzburger, "Jewish Ethics," 124.

66. See "Morality and Pessimism" and "Public and Private Morality," in *Public and Private Morality,* ed. Stuart Hampshire (Cambridge: Cambridge University Press, 1978), 1–53. Cf. also Isaiah Berlin, *The Crooked Timber of Humanity* (New York: Random House, 1992), 1–48.

67. B. Bava Metzia 30a.

68. B. Berakhot 19b and Menachot 37b. Rabbi Joseph B. Soloveitchik has pointed out in his *Yemei Hazikaron,* trans. Mosheh Kroneh (Jerusalem: World Zionist Organization, 1986), 9–11, that the Rabbinic notion of *kevod ha'beriot* is the equivalent of the biblical doctrine that human beings are endowed with the *Tzelem E-lohim* (the image of God). See also the illuminating discussion of *Kevod Haberiot* in Spero, *Halakhah,* 159–165.

69. Deut. 17:11.

70. Prov. 21:30 as quoted in B. Berakhot 19b. The Palestinian Talmud (Berakhot 3:3), however, can be interpreted as condoning violations even of Torah ordinances when warranted by considerations pertaining to *kevod ha'beriot.* While operating with the limitations that the Babylonian Talmud imposes upon the range of applicability of *kevod ha'beriot,* the medieval exegete Rabbeinu Asher (Rosh) states that the requirement to remove a forbidden garment in public applies only when the wearer himself becomes aware that he is wearing a *sha'atnez* garment. But there is no requirement that another party inform the person that the garment worn is prohibited because of *sha'atnez.* Maimonides, however, disagrees with this opinion and rules that under such circumstances one must inform the wearer. See *Tur Yoreh Deah,* 303.

71. *Ha'amek Davar,* Exod. 19:6.

72. Nachmanides, Torah Commentary to Deut. 6:18.

73. Ibid., Lev. 19:2.

74. *Maggid Mishneh,* Hilkhot Shekhenim 14:5.

75. Joseph Albo, *Sefer Ha-Ikkarim, Book of Principles,* critically edited on the basis

of manuscripts and old editions and provided with a translation and notes by Isaac Husik (Philadelphia: The Jewish Publication Society, 1930), vol. 3, chap. 23, 203.

76. See Paul Tillich, *Morality and Beyond* (New York: Harper and Row, 1963), 65–81. See also Michael Wyschogrod, "Judaism and Conscience," in *Standing Before God: Studies on Prayers in Scripture and in Tradition with Essays in Honor of John M. Oestreicher,* ed. Asher Finkel and Lawrence Zizzel (New York: Ktav, 1981), 313–328.

77. Michael Walzer, *Obligations: Essays on Disobedience, War and Citizenship* (Cambridge, Mass.: Harvard University Press, 1970), 121.

78. Mic. 6:8.

79. See Emil L. Fackenheim, "The Revealed Morality of Judaism and Modern Thought" in *Quest for Past and Future* (Bloomington: Indiana University Press, 1968), 204–228.

80. *Emunot Ve'deot,* chap. 3.

81. *Chovot Halevavot,* Introduction.

82. Meiri, Commentary to B. Shabbat 105b.

83. See my essay, "Samson Raphael Hirsch's Doctrine of Inner Revelation," in *From Ancient Israel to Modern Judaism: Intellect in Quest of Understanding. Essays in Honor of Marvin Fox,* ed. Jacob Neusner, Ernest S. Frerichs, and Nahum M. Sarna (Atlanta: Scholars Press, 1989), 4:3–11.

84. See Wurzburger, "Moral Society," 51.

85. Ibid., 46. It should be noted that B. Succah 32b invokes the verse "love ye truth and peace" (Zechariah 8:19) as an additional hermeneutical principle.

86. B. Berakhot 19b; Eruvin 53a; Sanhedrin 82a; Shavuot 30b.

87. For the notion of *Hora'at Sha'ah* (temporary suspension of the law), see B. Berakhot 54b, 63a; Yoma 69b; Yevamot 90b; Horiot 6a. See also Maimonides, M. T. Hilkhot Mamrim 2:4.

88. B. Nazir 23b; Horiot 10b.

89. Cf. Rabbi Chaim of Volozin, *Nefesh Hachayim,* chap. 7. For additional references, see Wurzburger, "Covenantal Imperatives," 8, n. 22.

CHAPTER TWO

1. I do not recall when I heard this comment by Rabbi Soloveitchik.

2. B. Bava Metzia 30b.

3. See Wurzburger, "Covenantal Imperatives," 3–12.

4. Martin Buber, in *Franz Rosenzweig, On Jewish Learning,* ed. N. N. Glatzer (New York: Schocken Books, 1965), 111.

5. Paul Tillich, *Systematic Theology* (Chicago: University of Chicago Press, 1971), 1:85.

6. See *The Writings of Martin Buber,* ed. Will Herberg (New York: Meridian Books, 1956), 43–62, 266–280. See also *On Judaism by Martin Buber,* ed. Nahum N. Glatzer (New York: Schocken, 1967), 214–225. See also my critique of Buber in "Covenantal Imperatives," 5–6.

7. See Fromm, *Gods,* and Hans Jonas, *The Imperative of Responsibility* (Chicago: University of Chicago Press, 1984).

8. Justice Oliver Wendell Holmes, quoted by Richard A. Posner, *The Problem of Jurisprudence,* (Cambridge, Mass.: Harvard University Press, 1990), 192.

9. See William D. Ross, *The Right and the Good* (Oxford: Clarendon Press, 1953).

10. According to the textual emendation of the *Tosefta* by Elijah Gaon of Vilna, even R. Yishmael concurs that the two expressions are employed to stress the importance of appearances. According to this reading, the disagreement between R. Akiva and Rabbi Yishmael does not involve substantive issues but relates only to the terminological question as to which of the two expressions refers to the need to appear correct even in the eyes of man. See Sifrei to Deuteronomy, Piska 79 and Piska 96 and Tosefta Shekalim 2:3.

11. See Peter Geach, *The Virtues* (Cambridge: Cambridge University Press, 1977); Philippa Foot, *Virtues and Vices* (Berkeley: University of California Press, 1978); Alasdair MacIntyre, *After Virtue* (Notre Dame: University of Notre Dame Press, 1981); Joseph Pieper, *The Four Cardinal Virtues* (Notre Dame: University of Notre Dame Press, 1966); Gilbert C. Meilander, *The Theory and Practice of Virtue,* (Notre Dame: University of Notre Dame Press, 1984); Stanley Hauerwas, *A Community of Character* (Notre Dame: University of Notre Dame Press, 1981). See also my discussion of agent-morality in chap. 5 of this book.

12. See chap. 6 for a more extensive discussion of this issue.

13. *Encyclopedia of Psychology,* 1972, vol. 2, *s.v.* "James-Lange theory of emotion."

14. Genesis Rabbah 44:1.

15. See *Ha'amek Davar,* Preface to Book of Genesis.

16. Joseph B. Soloveitchik, *Shiurim le-Zeikher Abba Mori,* (Jerusalem, 1986), 2:19.

17. Oral lecture delivered by Rabbi Soloveitchik. See above, chap. 1, n. 32.

18. For Maimonides' views on morality, see M. T. Hilkhot Deot.

19. Ibid. 6:2.

CHAPTER THREE

1. Maimonides, "Eight Chapters," chap. 4.

2. B. Gittin 59b. See also *Encyclopaedia Talmudit,* vol. 7, *s.v.* "Darkhei Shalom." See also Walter S. Wurzburger, "Darkhei Shalom," in *Gesher* (New York: Student Organization of Yeshiva Rabbi Isaac Elchanan Theological Seminary, 1978), 80–86. Portions of my treatment of *darkhei shalom* in this chapter are based upon material presented there.

3. See above, the reference to "the ways of peace" in the discussion of conscience, chap. 1.

4. For a thorough and comprehensive treatment of the subject, see Aaron Kirschenbaum, *Equity in Jewish Law: Halakhic Perspectives,* (New York and Hoboken: Ktav and Yeshiva University Press, 1991), 151–183.

5. See Bahya Ben Asher Ben Chlava, Commentary on Deuteronomy, Preface to *Shoftim.*

6. See *Derech Eretz Zuta, Perek Hashalom; Bamidbar Rabbah* 48:1 and *Devarim Rabbah* 5:14; *Midrash Tanchuma, Shoftim,* 13.

7. B. Berakhot 64a.

8. For a thorough discussion of this controversial issue, see Chaim Chizkiyahu Medini, *Sedei Chemed* (Warsaw, 1891), 1:79, 279–280.

9. Zohar, Numbers, 176.

10. J. Sotah 1:4; B. Sukkah 53b.

11. B. Sabbath 55a.

12. B. Yevamot 55b; Bava Metzia 23b.

13. See B. Bava Metzia 23b and 24a. See also Tosafot, B. Bava Metzia 23b, *s.v.* "Be'ushpisa." It should be noted that Rashi's restrictive definition of the meaning of peace is also followed in his commentary on B. Shabbat 126a, where he makes a sharp distinction between *gemilut chassadim* (acts of benevolence) and activities falling under the rubric of *hava'at shalom* (promotion of peace). Rabbeinu Nissim Bar Reuven of Girondi *ad locum* also operates with Rashi's approach. Meiri, however, adopting a slightly different version of the talmudic text, maintains that the promotion of peace represents an act of benevolence. For a thorough discussion of this issue, see Joseph D. Epstein, *Mitzvot Ha-shalom* (New York: Torat Ha-Adam Institute, 1969), 553–555.

14. B. Gittin 59b.

15. Moritz Lazarus, *Die Ethik des Judentums* (Frankfurt: J. Kaufmann, 1904), 1:181–183.

16. Lev. 25:3–46; Deut. 6:1–3, 9–16, 10:12–22, 11:13–28, 28:1–69, 29:9–28, 32:1–47.

17. Maimonides, *Guide*, Part 3, chap. 27. Reprinted by permission of New York University Press from *The Ethical Writings of Maimonides*, edited by Raymond L. Weiss with Charles E. Butterworth, copyright © 1975 by New York University, p. 139.

18. Maimonides, Commentary to Mishnah, Peah 1:1.

19. Maimonides, M. T., *Hilkhot Rotzeach* 4:8–9.

20. Yehudah Halevi, *Sefer ha-Kuzari*, part III, 7–9, 11, 32.

21. See Nachmanides, Torah Commentary to Deut. 7:12 and Lev. 18:4.

22. Avot 1:2.

23. Ibid. 1:18.

24. *Tur Choshen Mishpat*, Section 1.

25. Yehudah Halevi, *Sefer ha-Kuzari*, chap. 11, 48.

26. See Bahya Ben Asher, *Kad Ha-kemach, s.v.* "Tzitzit," in *Kol Kitvei Rabbeinu Bechayeh,* ed. Chaim Dov Chavel, (Jerusalem: Mossad Harav Kook, 1969), 183.

27. Albo, *Sefer Ha-Ikkarim* 1:5.

28. See *Meshekh Chakhmah,* Commentary to Exod. 14:14. Cf. also Maimonides, *Hilkhot Rotzeach* 4:9.

29. J. Nedarim 9:4.

30. B. Bava Kamma 20b.

31. Avot 5:10.

32. Ezekiel 16:49.

33. See Adin Steinsaltz, *A Reference Guide, The Talmud, Steinsaltz Edition* (New York: Random House, 1989), 215.

An excellent treatment of the relationship between formal legal obligations and purely moral requirements is found in Aaron Kirschenbaum's *Equity in Jewish Law/ Beyond Equity: Halakhic Aspirationism in Jewish Civil Law* (Hoboken and New York: Ktav and Yeshiva University Press, 1991), xxi–lxi, 1–135.

34. Deut. 22:34; Exod. 23:4–5.

35. Maimonides, Mishnah Commentary, Nedarim 4:4.

36. I am following the traditional interpretation of Lev. 19:16, which was adopted by the translator of the 1955 edition of *The Holy Scriptures* (Philadelphia: The Jewish Publication Society). Actually, the biblical text (Lev. 19:16) is ambiguous and can be interpreted in a variety of ways. Targum Onkelos and Ibn Ezra

interpret the biblical text as a prohibition against joining forces with murderers. See Aaron Kirschenbaum, "The 'Good Samaritan' in Jewish Law," *Dinei Yisrael* (1976): 7–85 and *The JPS Torah Commentary, Leviticus,* Commentary by Baruch A. Levine (Philadelphia: The Jewish Publication Society, 1989), 129.

37. B. Ketuvot 103a; Bava Batra 12b and 59a. Maimonides, M. T. *Hilkhot Shekheinim* 12:1–3 and *Shulchan Arukh, Choshen Mishpat* 174:1. See also Menachem Elon, *Jewish Law,* 4 vols. (Philadelphia: The Jewish Publication Society, 1994), 625–626.

38. B. Ketuvot 68a.

39. B. Shabbat 139a. See also R. Shneur Zalman of Liadi, *Likutei Amarim [Tanya],* chap. 32 and *Iggeret Hakodesh,* chaps. 5–6.

40. See Paul Tillich, *Love, Power and Justice* (London: Oxford University Press, 1954).

41. See Maimonides, *Hilkhot De'ot* 6:7–8. For an extensive discussion of the subject, see Rav Simcha Kook, "The Commandment of Rebuke — Privately and Publicly," in *Crossroads: Halachah and the Modern World* (Alon Shvut–Gush Etzion: Zomet Institute, 1990), 3:122–143.

42. See Mishnah Gittin, chap. 5.

43. Prov. 3:17. See also above, n. 3.

44. B. Gittin 59a–b.

45. Ibid., 61a.

46. David Hoffmann, *Der Schulchan Aruch und die Rabbiner uber das Verhaltniss der Juden zu Anderglaubigen* (Berlin: Judische Presse, 1894), 48–50.

47. See above, n. 15, of this chapter.

48. Jacob Z. Lauterbach, *Rabbinical Essays* (Cincinnati: Hebrew Union College Press, 1951), 292, n. 83.

49. See above, n. 15.

50. It should be noted that, although there are some exceptions, the term *eivah* does not occur in the Mishnah or Tosefta. It usually is employed in the Gemara when Amoraim seek to explain the reasons for decrees enacted by the Tannaim.

51. See the conflicting opinions cited by Moses Isserles, *Darkhei Mosheh,* subcommentary to *Tur Shulchan Arukh Yoreh Deah,* section 251. See also Joshua Wolk Katz, *Derishah, ad loc.*

52. Joseph Kapach, in *Commentary to Mishneh Torah* (Kiriat Uno: Makhon Mishnat Harambam, 1984), 1:538, n. 17, disagrees with my position. He contends that, according to Maimonides, only Jewish communal institutions are required to give charity to non-Jews, since overt discriminatory policies would adversely affect the welfare of the Jewish community. In the case of individuals' distributing their own personal funds, the situation is different. An individual's failure to assist any particular non-Jew would not provoke animosity against the Jewish community.

I believe that the textual material on which Kapach bases his opinion lends itself to a different interpretation, which would not do violence to the ethical thrust of the Maimonidean conception of *darkhei shalom.* The words *bikhlal* as well as *im* could be interpreted, following the approach of Rabbeinu Nissim Ben Reuven Gerondi *ad* B.T., Gittin 61a, as merely suggesting that with respect to charity and other acts of benevolence we have the same obligation toward non-Jews as toward Jews. See also *Beur Hagra* to *Yoreh Deah,* 251, n. 2. For reasons indicated later in this chapter, as well as my overall approach to Maimonidean ethics (chap. 5 of this volume), I feel constrained to reject any interpretation of Maimonides' position that fails to do justice to his espousal of agent-morality.

53. Prov. 3:17.

54. M.T. Hilkhot Avadim 9:8.

55. That Maimonides quotes this verse from Psalms, which in M.T. Hilkhot Avadim is cited in connection with the imperative to imitate the divine moral attributes, is in itself convincing evidence that, for Maimonides, *darkhei shalom* is grounded in agent-morality. While act-morality may differentiate between obligations toward Jews and toward those who are not included in the Covenantal community, agent-morality does not make any distinction.

56. M.T. Hilkhot Avodah Zarah 10:8.

57. As previously mentioned, in chap. 1, n. 47, Rabbi Chaim David Halevi argues that the obligation to practice charity toward non-idolatrous non-Jews is not at all related to considerations involving *darkhei shalom,* but is based on a general ethical obligation. I thoroughly disagree with this position, because, according to Maimonides, all ethical obligations must derive their normative authority from a divine commandment. My own position is much closer to that of Rabbi Issar Yehudah Unterman, as expressed in *Morashah* 1:5–10. I do not find the arguments adduced by Rabbi Halevi (n. 8) against Rabbi Unterman's position to be convincing.

To be sure, Rabbi Unterman does not operate with my distinction between act-morality and agent-morality. In chap. 5 of this volume, I demonstrate that the Maimonidean doctrine mandating the practice of philanthropy toward non-Jews reflects considerations of agent-morality.

58. Abraham of Posquiere, in his *Hasagot (ad loc.),* takes a far more lenient position than does Maimonides.

CHAPTER FOUR

1. B. Sanhedrin 46a.

2. See B. Kiddushin 40b; Pesikta Zutrati to Ekev.

3. Ephraim E. Urbach, *Chazal: Emunot Vedeot* (Jerusalem, Magnes Press, 1969), 392–396.

4. Genesis Rabbah 9:10.

5. For an extensive discussion of the problem of evil, see David Birnbaum, *God and Evil* (New York: Ktav, 1989).

6. See Emil Fackenheim, *God's Presence in History* (New York: New York University Press, 1970); Eliezer Berkovits, *Faith After the Holocaust* (New York: Ktav, 1973). I have dealt with this issue in my article, "Theological and Philosophical Responses to the Holocaust," in *Issues in Teaching the Holocaust: A Guide,* ed. Robert Hirt and Thomas Kessner (New York: Yeshiva University, 1981), 27–32. I wish to call attention to the following excerpt: "It might therefore be useful to refer to Professor Plantinga's thesis, that once the existence of God is accepted as an article of faith rather than an empirical hypothesis postulated to explain the goodness of the universe, one can dispose of the arguments from evil in a relatively simple manner. Unless one bases one's argument for the existence of God on natural theology and postulates the existence of God as an explanatory hypothesis to account for the harmonious structure and order of the universe, one need not pretend to know the answer as to why any particular evil is really necessary for the existence

of the greatest possible good. It suffices to assert that from a Divine perspective, whatever evil exists must be necessary. But there is no need for our finite limited understanding to fathom the reasons why without a particular evil the greatest possible good could not have been attained." See also my contribution to *Teaching the Holocaust: An Exploration of the Problem* (New York: Stone-Saperstein Center for Jewish Education, 1976), 24–32, as well as my essay in the *1982 Theology Roundtable: Theodicy* (New York: The 92nd Street Y, 1982) and my discussion of the problem of evil in "Orthodox Judaism and Human Purpose," in *Religion and Human Purpose,* ed. T. Horosz and T. Clements (Dordrecht: Martinus Nijhoff, 1986), 106–108.

7. See Joseph B. Soloveitchik, "Kol Dodi Dofek," in *Besod Hayachid Vehayachad,* ed. Pinchas Peli (Jerusalem: Orot, 1976).

8. It should be noted, however, that Rashi stresses the beneficial consequences of illness, because it is conducive to engendering repentance and contrition. Commenting on the statement of the Babylonian Talmud that "the Sages approved of King Hezekiah's hiding of the Book of Medicines" (Pesachim 56a), Rashi cites as reason for their positive response, "because the heart of the sick would not be subdued as the result of their immediate recovery." In his opinion, the instantaneous cure deprived the patient of the spiritual benefits that would have been derived from a longer illness. Maimonides, on the other hand, emphasizes in his Mishnah Commentary (Pesachim 4:9), that the reason for the Sages' endorsement of the king's actions had nothing to do with the effectiveness of the medicines, but, on the contrary, was due to the fact that the reliance on the quack medicines contained in the "Book of Medicines" represented a serious health hazard. Maimonides regards it as axiomatic that a religious responsibility exists to do everything within one's power to cure individuals as expeditiously as possible.

9. B. Ketuvot 60a.

10. B. Berakhot 63a; Nedarim 9b and 10a; Nazir 3b, 19a, and 22a. Significantly, Rashi (Torah Commentary to Num. 6:11) cites the opinion of R. Eleazar Hakapar. The reason a sacrifice of a sin offering is required upon the expiration of the period during which the special restrictions imposed upon the Nazarite were in effect, is due to the fact that to deny oneself the enjoyment of wine was in itself a sin. An entirely different approach is adopted by Nachmanides (Torah Commentary to Num. 6:11). In his view, the sin offering was mandated because "having attained the level of holiness of a Nazarite . . . it would have been appropriate for him to remain the rest of his life in the state of a Nazarite consecrated to his God . . . And he requires now atonement for reverting to a stage where he is defiled with the appetites of the world." See also Torah Commentary of R. Bechayeh to Num. 6:13.

11. B. Chagigah 9b; Pesachim 50b; Taanit 15a; Nedarim 81a; Exodus Rabbah 31:3; Leviticus Rabbah 13:4.

12. "One should not spend more than one fifth lest one [become so impoverished] that one would require the assistance of others" (B. Ketuvot 50a).

13. Hilkhot Arakhim Ve-charamim 8:12.

14. Reprinted by permission of Kluwer Academic Publishers from my article, "Orthodox Judaism and Human Purpose," in Horosz and Clements, *Religion and Human Purpose,* 115–116.

15. B. Shabbat 92a; Nedarim 38a.

16. Leviticus Rabbah, 34:10. Cf. also B. Bava Batra 10a.

17. According to Deut. 15:11, no amount of human effort will succeed in completely solving the problem of poverty. But this does not diminish our responsibility to do our utmost to alleviate the misery caused by it.

18. See the illuminating discussion of the different perspectives on the practice of charity in the chapter "From Charity to Philanthropy," in Daniel J. Boorstin, *Hidden History* (New York: Vintage Books, 1989), 193–209.

19. B. Bava Batra 10a.

20. Avot 4:16.

21. Ibid. 4:17.

22. Ibid.

23. See Wurzburger, "Orthodox Judaism and Human Purpose," iii. Cf. also my essay, "The Jewish Attitude towards Psychedelic Religion," in *Judaism and Drugs*, ed. Leo Landman (New York: Commission of Synagogue Relations, Federations of Jewish Philanthropies, 1973), 139–143.

24. M.T. Hilkhot Deot 1:12. Reprinted by permission of New York University Press from *The Ethical Writings of Maimonides*, edited by Raymond L. Weiss with Charles E. Butterworth, copyright © 1975 by New York University, p. 30.

25. Ibid. 6:6. Reprinted by permission of New York University Press from *The Ethical Writings of Maimonides*, edited by Raymond L. Weiss with Charles E. Butterworth, copyright © 1975 by New York University, p. 48.

26. Ibid. 6:7. Reprinted by permission of New York University Press from *The Ethical Writings of Maimonides*, edited by Raymond L. Weiss with Charles E. Butterworth, copyright © 1975 by New York University, p.48.

27. Commentary to Mishnah, Avot 3:15 and Introduction to chap. 10 of Sanhedrin. M.T. Hilkhot Teshuvah, chaps. 9–10.

28. M.T., Laws of Repentance 10:6–9. See also his Mishnah Commentary, Sanhedrin, chap. 10. Nachmanides also shares this perspective and looks upon religious performance that is totally devoid of any interest in spiritual rewards as the ideal form of piety. Cf. Torah Commentary to Exod. 20:6 and Deut. 6:7.

29. Saadiah, *Emunot Vedeot* 9:2.

30. Significantly, the above-cited Mishnah, "the reward of a mitzvah is a mitzvah," is interpreted by Arama in a radically different manner from that of Maimonides. He regards the awareness of the ensuing beneficial consequences of a mitzvah as an indispensable component of the mitzvah, since he maintains that unless there are sanctions, one cannot speak of law. See Sarah Heller Wilensky, *R. Yitzchak Arama U'mishnato* (Jerusalem: Bialik Institute, 1956), 215–216.

31. Avot 1:3.

32. Sifrei, Ekev, 48. Cf. also B. Nedarim 62a.

33. J. Nedarim 9:4.

34. Ohalot 7:6; Terumot 8:12.

35. Maimonides, M.T. Yesodei Hatorah 5:5.

36. See Nachum L. Rabinovitch, "What is the Halakhah for Organ Transplants?" *Tradition* 9, 4, (1968): 20–27; Yitzchak Liebes, "Be'inyan Hashtalat Ha'eivarim," *Noam* 14 (1971), 28–111. See also Basil F. Herring, *Jewish Ethics and Halakhah for Our Times* (Hoboken and New York: Ktav and Yeshiva University Press, 1989), 2:85–131.

37. Yoreh Deah 339:1. See also Immanuel Jakobovits, *Jewish Medical Ethics* (New York: Bloch, 1959), 121–125.

38. Gen. 1:27.

39. Mishnah, Sanhedrin 4:5.

40. Even Maimonides, while balking at all anthropocentric formulations, nevertheless maintains that among terrestrial creatures, only human beings can come under the aegis of the Special Divine Providence. All other terrestrial creatures are only subject to the General Providence, which is exercised through the operation of the natural laws governing the various species (*Guide* 3:17). In a similar vein, Joseph Albo (*Sefer Ha-Ikkarim,* 3:12) declares that while for animals divine providence is only concerned with the species, human beings are singled out for special treatment so that all individuals may receive reward or punishment in accordance with their deserts.

41. See Robert Nozick, *Anarchy, State and Utopia,* (New York: Basic Books, 1974), 35–47.

42. For an illuminating discussion of this issue, see Ovadyah Yoseph, "Teshuvah Beheter Hashtalat Kelayah," *Dinei Yisrael* 7 (1976), 26–43.

43. Deut. 15:8.

44. B. Ketuvot 67a. See also Daniel Lander, "Be'inyan Chiuv Dai Machsoro," in *Sefer Kavod Harav,* ed. Moshe D. Sherman (New York: Student Organization of Yeshiva, 1984), 202–205.

45. Mosheh Tzvi Neheria, "Tzedakah Shel Chessed u'Tzedakah shel Mishpat," in *Sefer Hazikaron Le'Avraham Spiegelman,* ed. Aryeh Morgenstern (Jerusalem: Moreshet, 1979), 71–80.

46. Robert Nozick, *Philosophical Explanations* (Cambridge, Mass.: Harvard University Press, 1981), 401ff.

47. Naturally, priority should be assigned to meet real needs rather than enabling individuals to indulge in luxuries they can no longer afford. Obviously, one should not spend charity dollars on furnishing luxury cars, if it is at the expense of other really destitute individuals, who lack basic necessities. But this is merely a matter of priorities, not principles. In theory, any act designed to supply a felt need of a fellow human being represents a benevolent act.

48. Aharon Lichtenstein, "Se'od Tisod Imo: Hishtatfut Hamekabel Bi'gemilut Chassadim," in *Sefer Hazikaron Le'Avraham Spiegelman,* 81–93.

49. B. Sukkah 49b.

50. B. Bava Metzia 66b. See also Rashi to Gen. 18:1.

51. Yitzhak Twersky, "On Law and Ethics in the Mishneh Torah: A Case Study of Hilkhot Megillah 11:17," *Tradition* 24, 2 (Winter 1989): 138–149. See, especially, p. 249, n. 25.

52. Samson R. Hirsch, *Horeb,* trans. Dayan Dr. I. Grunfeld (London: Soncino Press, 1981), 427. For a thorough analysis of the entire subject, see the invaluable article of Isadore Twersky, "Some Aspects of the Jewish Attitude Towards the Welfare State," *Tradition* 5, 2 (Spring 1962): 137–158.

53. Reprinted by permission of New York University Press from *The Ethical Writings of Maimonides,* edited by Raymond L. Weiss with Charles E. Butterworth, copyright © 1975 by New York University, p. 147.

54. Exod. 34:6–7.

55. I completely disagree with the view of a number of scholars who argue that the Maimonidean ideal, as described in part III, chap. 54 of the *Guide,* refers exclusively to the political function of the prophet. In my study, "The Centrality of

Virtue-Ethics in Maimonides," in *Of Scholars, Savants and their Texts, Studies in Philosophy and Religious Thought, Essays in Honor of Arthur Hyman,* ed. Ruth Link-Salinger, (New York: Peter Lang, 1989), 251–260, I have stated my reasons for adopting the approach of Professor Twersky, who maintains that the ideal of *imitatio dei* as formulated in the last chapter of the *Guide* is not reserved for the statesman but is addressed to every individual who has acquired philosophical understanding.

Maimonides, of course, indicates (*Guide* 1:54) that *some* of the thirteen attributes have relevance only as models for the statesman. But this by no means implies that the others are also irrelevant to the quest of *imitatio dei* on the part of individuals without political responsibility. See, especially, my study, "The Centrality," 260, n. 23.

56. B. Kiddushin 76b.

57. Maimonides, M.T. Hilkhot Matenot Ani'im 10:4. Cf. also B. Bava Batra 8a and 10b.

58. B. Pesachim 8a; Rosh Hashanah 4a; Bava Batra 10b.

59. B. Ta'anit 9a. See also notes of Rema (R. Mosheh Isserles) to Shulchan Arukh, Yoreh Deah 247:4. For a wide-ranging discussion of the extent to which purely selfish motives may be acceptable in philanthropy, see Medini, *Sedei Chemed,* 5:150–152.

60. In his *Beth Halevi,* 1863–64, (vol. 2, "Derush 1") R. Yoseph Dov Ber Soloveitchik called attention to the two distinct components of the commandment of giving charity.

CHAPTER FIVE

1. See Introduction, n. 4.

2. Abraham Joshua Heschel, *God in Search of Man: A Philosophy of Judaism* (New York: Farrar, Strauss, Giroux, 1955), 320.

3. 1 Sam. 16:7.

4. Exod. 20:14.

5. Lev. 19:17.

6. Ibid. 19:18.

7. Abraham Ibn Ezra, Torah Commentary to Exod. *ad* Exod. 20:14.

8. Exod. 20:2.

9. Maimonides, M.T. Hilkhot Yesodei ha-Torah 1:1–6.

10. *Harav Joseph Dov Soloveitchik Halevi al Ha'teshuvah,* ed. Pinchas Peli (Jerusalem: World Zionist Organization, 1974), 195–198.

11. I have discussed the originality of Maimonides' conception that the cultivation of desirable traits of character is a specific religious commandment in my "Centrality," 251–260. See also Yitzhak Twersky, "On Law and Ethics in the Mishneh Torah; A Case Study of Hilkhot Megillah II:17," *Tradition* 24, 2 (1989): 138–149.

12. R. Chaim Vital, *Shaarey Kedushah* 1:2.

13. Maimonides, M.T. Hilkhot De'ot 1:6.

14. Avot 5:23.

15. Maimonides, "Eight Chapters," Introduction to Avot, chap. 6.

16. Professor Isadore Twersky [*Introduction to the Code of Maimonides,* Yale Judaica Series, vol. 22 (New Haven and London: Yale University Press, 1980), 453–459] argues that the opinion expressed by Maimonides in his Commentary on the Mish-

nah represented only his early view, which was subsequently abandoned when he composed his more mature and authoritative *magnum opus*, the *Mishneh Torah*. Professor Twersky bases his position largely upon the statement in *Hilkhot Teshuvah* (7:4), where Maimonides maintains that the greater the effort required to repress sinful tendencies, the greater the spiritual stature of the individual. It would therefore follow, so Professor Twersky contends, that an individual who has to expend effort to overcome undesirable traits of character in order to perform meritorious actions should be regarded as superior to an individual who performs meritorious actions effortlessly, without any need to struggle against natural inclinations.

It seems to me, however, that there is considerable evidence that in the *Code,* Maimonides still adhered to his early view concerning the spiritual superiority of the individual with desirable traits of character. It is significant that in *Hilkhot Teshuvah* (7:3) he asserts that repentance is needed especially for wrong dispositions, not merely for wrong actions.

On the basis of this evidence I am persuaded that although with respect to the merit of the action itself, greater reward is due to the individual who must repress his inclinations, on balance, the virtuous individual is superior, because the mere possession of an undesirable trait of character constitutes a violation of the imperative "Thou shalt walk in His ways." See Wurzburger, "Centrality," 251–260.

17. Eliezer Schweid, *Iyunim Bishemoneh Perakim le-Rambam* (Jerusalem: Jewish Agency, 1969), 105–119.

18. Marvin Fox, *Interpreting Maimonides: Studies in Methodology, Metaphysics and Moral Philosophy* (Chicago: University of Chicago, 1990), 93–122.

19. Nozick, *Philosophical Explanations*, 401ff.

20. Sifrei, Ekev, 49.

21. M.T. Hilkhot De'ot 1:10. Reprinted by permission from New York University Press from *The Ethical Writings of Maimonides,* edited by Raymond L. Weiss with Charles E. Butterworth, copyright © 1975 by New York University, p. 30.

22. Ibid.

23. B. Sotah 14a.

24. See Wurzburger, "Centrality"; *idem,* "Law, Philosophy and *Imitatio Dei* in Maimonides," *Aquinas* 30 (1987): 27–34; and *idem, "Imitatio Dei* in Maimonides' Sefer Hamitzvot and the Mishneh Torah," in *Tradition and Transition,* ed. Jonathan Sacks (London: Jews' College Press, 1986), 321–324.

In his *Pachad Yitzchak, Sha'ar U'veyom Hashabat* (Brooklyn: Gur Aryeh Institute, 1982), 226–227, R. Yitzchak Hutner offers a different explanation why, in the *Code,* Maimonides does not utilize the commandment "Thou shalt walk in His ways" as a prooftext for the requirement to practice lovingkindness. I believe, however, that the weight of the evidence supports my view that Maimonides abandoned his earlier view as formulated in the *Sefer Hamitzvot.*

25. Avot 3:15.

26. Professor Twersky in "On Law and Ethics," p. 149, n. 25, called attention to the fact that acts of *chesed* are classified at times by Maimonides not as commandments regulating our acts toward our fellow man but as commandments between man and God.

27. Reprinted by permission of New York University Press from *The Ethical Writings of Maimonides,* edited by Raymond L. Weiss with Charles E. Butterworth,

copyright © 1975 by New York University, p. 30. It should, however, be noted that in chap. 7 of *Hilkhot De'ot*, Maimonides extolls a recommended character trait as an instrumental *social* value conducive "to the settlement of the earth and proper social relations among human beings." While this seems to contradict our thesis that *Hilkhot De'ot* is not concerned with interpersonal relations as such, it should be borne in mind that in the Introduction to the *Ethical Writings of Maimonides* (p. 4 and n. 4 on p. 25), Raymond L. Weiss observes that the cultivation of the proper dispositions is designed to settle the human mind so that, provided the proper intellectual faculties are developed, the individual will be qualified to engage in metaphysical contemplation.

28. M.T. Hilkhot De'ot, 6, 3.

For a somewhat different approach to the solution of the seeming contradiction in Maimonides' opinion on the obligation to love non-observant Jews, see Norman Lamm, *Halakhot Ve'Halikhot* (Jerusalem: Mosad Harav Kook, 1990), 149–158.

29. See my article on "Darkhei Shalom," 80–86.

30. See my "Centrality," p. 258, and Isadore Twersky, "Welfare State."

31. M.T. Hilkhot Teshuvah 3:7.

32. Hilkhot Teshuvah 7:3.

33. It is in this light that we can appreciate Maimonides' insistence that the determination as to whether individuals or communities are judged as righteous or wicked does not depend upon the numerical balance of *mitzvot* over transgressions, but largely upon qualitative factors known only to God (M.T. Hilkhot Teshuvah 3:2). This contrasts with the position of Saadiah (*Emunot ve'De'ot* 5:2), who considers only quantitative factors.

34. Deut. 13:5. According to Ibn Ezra, cleaving to God is not a commandment but the assurance that as the result of proper conduct one will eventually reach a state of attachment to God. For alternate interpretations, see also Nachmanides, Torah Commentary, Deut. 6:13, 11:22, and 13:5.

35. B. Ketuvot, 111b.

36. M.T. Hilkhot De'ot 6:3.

37. M.T. Hilkhot De'ot 6:2.

38. See Maimonides, "Eight Chapters," chap. 7.

39. M.T. Yesodei Hatorah 7:1.

40. See Maimonides, "Eight Chapters," chap. 7. Reprinted by permission of New York University Press from *The Ethical Writings of Maimonides*, edited by Raymond L. Weiss with Charles E. Butterworth, copyright © 1975 by New York University, p. 81.

41. B. Sabbath 133b.

42. Sifra to Lev. 19:2.

43. Lev. 19:2.

44. In his *Tiferet Yisrael*, R. Israel Lipschutz offers this comment on the first Mishnah of the tractate Avot: "It appears to me that the Mishnah starts with the acceptance of the Torah, lest a person think that to occupy oneself with Torah and its practice would be sufficient for the perfection of one's soul, and that even if one would not improve one's moral traits and dispositions, one might merit [the rewards] of the world-to-come. But this is not so, because the punishment for *middot* (traits of character) is severe (B. Yevamot 21a and Bava Batra 88b)."

The talmudic references cited by *Tiferet Yisrael,* however, have absolutely no bearing upon the requirement to cultivate virtues, since the term *middot* has a double meaning. It can refer to traits of character, but also to measures in the literal sense of the term. It is evident from the context of the talmudic statement, especially in the light of the biblical texts quoted, that *onshan shel middot* refers to the sin incurred by the possession of false weights and measures — not of undesirable traits of character. The other sources adduced by *Tiferet Yisrael,* however, support his thesis that the cultivation of desirable traits of character plays an important role in the Jewish scale of values. Cf. also his comments on Avot 2:1.

45. J. Kiddushin 4:1; B. Yevamot 79a; Nedarim 20a.

46. B. Beitzah 32b.

47. Avot 5:23. See also above, nn. 16 and 17. Both Professors Twersky and Schweid agree that this classical source does not differentiate between ethical and ritual laws with respect to the principle that the reward is commensurate with the effort.

48. See above, nn. 15, 16, and 47.

49. See the concluding chapter of the *Guide.*

50. I follow here largely the approach of Professor Twersky, who rejects the view of Professor Pines that the imitation of the divine moral perfections relates exclusively to the political function of the prophet. For a more extensive discussion of the topic, see my "Centrality."

51. See my treatment of this issue in "Law, Philosophy and *Imitatio Dei* in Maimonides," 31–32.

52. Nachmanides, Torah Commentary to Deut. 6:18.

53. Maimonides, M.T. Hilkhot Teshuvah 10:1–2.

54. Saadiah, *Emunot ve'Deot* 3:1.

55. Avot 4:2.

56. See above chap. 4, n. 33.

57. See Maimonides, "Eight Chapters," chap. 5, and M.T. Hilkhot De'ot 3:3.

58. Nicomachean Ethics, Book 2, chap. 6.

59. Maimonides, "Eight Chapters," chap. 4.

60. See Daniel H. Frank, "Humility as a Virtue," in *Moses Maimonides and His Time: Studies in Philosophy and the History of Philosophy,* vol. 19, ed. Eric L. Ormsby (Washington, D.C.: Catholic University of America Press, 1989).

61. See Moses David Gross, *Otzar Ha-Aggadah* (Jerusalem: Mossad Harav Kook, 1963), 1:149–51, 2:555–558.

62. Cf. Rabbeinu Yonah Gerundi's view (Commentary to Avot 2:1) that the middle road is recommended by the Tannaim as most conducive to the attainment of proper dispositions. In a similar way, he interprets the biblical verse (Prov. 4:26) as implying that we should seek the proper balance between the extremes.

63. M.T. Hilkhot De'ot 2:3. Reprinted by permission of New York University Press, from *The Ethical Writings of Maimonides,* edited by Raymond L. Weiss with Charles E. Butterworth, copyright © 1975 by New York University, p. 31.

64. Reprinted by permission of New York University Press, from *The Ethical Writings of Maimonides,* edited by Raymond L. Weiss with Charles E. Butterworth, copyright © 1975 by New York University, p. 29.

65. Ibid., 32.

66. Ibid.

67. Simon Rawidowicz, "'Mishneh Torah' Studies" (I–III), in *Metzudah* (London, 1954), 7:173ff.

68. See my "The Maimonidean Matrix of Rabbi Joseph B. Soloveitchik's Two-Tiered Ethics," in *Through the Sound of Many Voices,* ed. Jonathan V. Plaut (Toronto: Lester and Orpen Dennys Ltd., 1982), 172–183.

69. At the conclusion of M. T. Hilkhot De'ot, Maimonides employs the expression *"Yishuv Ha'aretz."*

70. B. Sanhedrin 24b.

71. M.T. Yesodei Hatorah 4:20; *Guide* 2:40.

72. M.T. Hilkhot De'ot 7:11.

73. See above, n. 60.

74. Steven Schwarzschild, "Moral Radicalism and 'Middlingness' in the Ethics of Maimonides," *Studies in Medieval Culture* II, (1977): 65–94.

75. See, especially, chap. I, p. 10.

76. Joseph B. Soloveitchik, "The Lonely Man of Faith," *Tradition* 7, 2 (1965): 5–67.

77. Joseph B. Soloveitchik, "Majesty and Humility," *Tradition* 17, 2 (Spring 1978): 25–37.

78. See my discussion in "Jewish Ethics," 126–127.

CHAPTER SIX

1. To be sure, secular ethical theories need not suffer from a monistic bias. They may also operate with a variety of incommensurable values, as evidenced by the writings of Stuart Hampshire and Bernard Williams.

2. See Wurzburger, "Jewish Ethics," 124.

3. See above, chap. 3.

4. B. Bava Metzia 23b–24a.

5. Exod. 34:7; Num. 14:18.

6. See Eliezer Ben Samuel of Metz, *Sefer Yere'im,* paragraph 261. His opinion is based on Sifra to Leviticus, Kedoshim 3:2, Piska 3.

7. B. Bava Metzia 44a.

8. For a comprehensive treatment of the subject, see Basil F. Herring, *Jewish Ethics,* 2:221–274.

There is only one minor objection I wish to raise with respect to a terminological issue. Rabbi Herring refers to the fact that sometimes there is reference to *Genevat Da'at,* whereas the biblical verse quoted refers to the "stealing of the heart." R. Herring observes that "the difference in phraseology is inconsequential" (p. 236). It should be pointed out, however, that, actually, in biblical Hebrew, the term *lev* (heart) frequently denotes the seat of the intellect (and not merely of the emotions) and, therefore, the stealing of the heart in biblical parlance is the equivalent of the Rabbinic expression "stealing of the mind."

9. Tosefta, Bava Kamma 7:3. Cf. Mekhilta, Mishpatim, 13.

10. Mishnah, Bava Metzia 4:11.

11. Mishnah, Bava Metzia 4:10.

12. Hilkhot Mekhirah 18:1–2.

13. B. Sanhedrin 74a.

14. See Jakobovits, *Jewish Medical Ethics*, 276.

15. Horiot 3:7.

16. See Daniel Callahan, *Setting Limits* (New York: Simon and Schuster, 1987). See also the illuminating discussion of the issue by Dan W. Brock in his article, "Justice, Healthcare and the Elderly," *Philosophy and Public Affairs* (Summer 1989), 297–312.

17. Abraham Yitzchak Hakohen Kook, *Mishpat Cohen* (Jerusalem: Mossad Harav Kook, 1985), 305–347. See also R. Yaakov Navon, "Risking Lives to Save Lives," in *Crossroads: Halachah and the Modern World* (Jerusalem: Zomet Institute, Alon Shevut Gush Etzion, 1990), 3:47–63, and R. Shaul Yisraeli, "Individual Life during Mass Rescue," in *Crossroads*, 3:65–73.

18. B. Sanhedrin 74b.

19. See Mordecai M. Kaplan, *The Purpose and Meaning of Jewish Existence: A People in the Image of God* (Philadelphia: The Jewish Publication Society, 1964), 178–199.

20. *Ahad Ha-am: Essays, Letters, Memoirs*, trans. from the Hebrew and ed. Leon Simon (Oxford: East and West Library, 1948), 130–137.

21. Glatzer, *On Judaism*, 108–148.

22. Kaplan, *Jewish Existence*, 178–199.

23. Exod. 19:6.

24. See William Kluback, *The Legacy of Hermann Cohen* (Atlanta: Scholars Press, 1989), 3. He calls attention to Kurt Lowith's statement that "only the Jews are a really historical people, constituted as such by religion, by the act of the Sinaitic revelation."

25. M.T., Hilkhot Teshuvah 3:11.

26. Ruth 1:16.

27. Stuart Hampshire, *Morality and Conflict*, (Cambridge, Mass.: Harvard University Press, 1983), 86–100.

28. See *Encyclopaedia Talmudit*, vol. 10, *s.v.* "Hefker Beth Din."

29. See Ross, *The Right and the Good*.

30. My approach differs from R. M. Hare, who in his *Moral Thinking* (Oxford: Clarendon Press, 1981) contends that in principle all ethical dilemmas are resolvable by recourse to a single criterion.

31. See my "Foundations of Jewish Ethics," 124.

32. Immanuel Kant, *On a Supposed Right to Tell Lies from Benevolent Motives,* quoted by Paul Dietrichson, "Kant's Criteria of Universalizability," in *Foundations of the Metaphysics of Morals with Critical Essays,* ed. Robert Paul Wolff (New York: Bobbs Merrill, 1969), 199.

33. Nachmanides, Torah Commentary, Lev. 19:17.

34. B. Bava Metzia 62a.

35. J. Ketuvot 11:3; B. Ketuvot 50a and 86a; cf. also Tosafot B.T. Kiddushin 32a, *s.v.* "oru leih." See also *Shulchan Arukh, Yoreh Deah* 251:3.

36. Isa. 58:7.

37. B.T. Bava Metzia 71a. See also *Shulchan Aruch, Yoreh Deah* 251:3.

38. See my "Foundations of Jewish Ethics," 124.

39. Bahya Ibn Pakuda, *Duties of the Heart,* chaps. 2–3.

40. Deut. 32:18.

41. B. Kiddushin 31b.

42. See my article, "Obligations Towards Aged Parents," in *The Jewish Woman in the Middle,* ed. Joseph Lowin, Hadassah Study Series (New York: Hadassah, 1984), 12–15.

43. See above, chap. 5, n. 78.

44. Ahad Ha'am, "Judaism and the Gospels," in *Nationalism and Jewish Ethics: Basic Writings of Ahad Ha'am,* ed. and intro. Hans Kohn (New York: Schocken Books, 1962), 301–302.

45. Deut. 16:20.

46. Ibid. 1:17.

47. Midrash Tanhuma Shoftim.

48. See Aaron Kirschenbaum, "Representation in Litigation in Jewish Law," *Dinei Yisrael* 6 (1975): 25–41; and Benjamin Lipkin, "Arikhat Din Be'Mishpat Hatorah," *Sinai* 31 (1953): 165–183. See also Herring, *Jewish Ethics,* 91–120.

For an invaluable treatment of the basic difference between the respective objectives of Jewish and secular law, see Mosheh Silberg, *Kach Darko Shel Talmud* (Jerusalem: Student Organization of the Hebrew University, 1961), 72.

49. Ahad Ha'am, "Judaism and the Gospels," in *Ten Essays on Zionism and Judaism,* trans. Leon Simon (New York: Arno Press, 1973), 223–253.

50. B.T. Bava Metzia 62a.

51. It is revealing that the most articulate critique of John Rawls's position has been provided by Robert Nozick, a renowned philosopher, who is deeply rooted in the Jewish tradition. In his *Anarchy, State and Utopia,* Nozick develops an antithetical conception of justice, which takes account of the historical factors that affect the justice of institutional arrangements. Whereas for Rawls the moral propriety of a social contract is completely determined by ahistorical factors, Nozick operates with a social contract doctrine, which, however fictitious, at least justifies the protection of property rights on the basis of historical entitlements.

52. See chap. 1, n. 78.

53. M.T. Hilkhot De'ot 1:5.

54. Rabbi Joseph B. Soloveitchik, *Halakhic Man,* trans. Lawrence Kaplan (Philadelphia: The Jewish Publication Society, 1983), 99–137.

55. Prayer Book, Weekday Amidah.

56. B. Shabbat 10a.

57. B. Makkot 23b.

58. Deut. 30:12. See also B.T. Bava Metzia 59b.

59. See R. Chaim of Volozin, *Nefesh ha-Chaim,* Part 4; and R. Naftali Tzvi Yehudah Berlin, *Ha'ameik Davar,* to Exod. 34:1. Cf. also R. Joseph B. Soloveitchik's essay, "Ish ha-Halakhah."

60. Ibn Ezra, Torah Commentary to Exod. 20:14.

61. Pakuda, *Duties,* chap. 4.

62. Num. 12:3.

63. B. Megillah 31a.

64. Soloveitchik, "Majesty and Humility," 25–37.

65. Avot 2:12; B. Berakhot 63a. See also Maimonides, M.T. Hilkhot De'ot 3:2, and "Eight Chapters," chap. 5.

66. Rabbi Chaim of Volozin, *Nefesh ha'Chayyim,* chap. 4.

67. I am indebted to Martin Buber and Gershom Scholem for this understanding of Jewish mysticism.

68. B. Berakhot 25b.

69. B. Shabbat 127a.

70. Exod. 18:15.

71. I have benefited enormously from Hans Jonas's brilliant analysis of the implications of the biblical doctrine of Creation in his essay, "Jewish and Christian Elements in Philosophy: Their Share in the Emergence of the Modern Mind," in *Philosophical Essays: From Ancient Creed to Technological Man* (Chicago: University of Chicago Press, 1974), 21–44.

72. Exod. 33:20.

73. Soloveitchik, "Lonely Man," 237–244.

74. Rabbi Chaim of Volozin, *Nefesh ha-Chaim*, chap. 1.

75. Mussaph service of Festivals.

76. Rabbi Chaim of Volozin, *Nefesh ha-Chaim*, 1:4.

77. Ps. 8:6–7.

78. See Soloveitchik, "Lonely Man," 5–67; and *idem*, "Majesty and Humility."

79. See my "Enlightenment and Emancipation," *Judaism* 38, 4 (Fall 1989), 407, and my "Confronting the Challenge of the Values of Modernity," *The Torah and Madda Journal* 1 (1989), 104–112.

80. *Sefer Ketav Sofer al Chamishah Chumshei Torah* (Tel Aviv: Sinai Publishing, 1980), 11b.

81. Nachmanides, Torah Commentary, Lev. 26:11.

82. Gershom Scholem, *The Messianic Idea in Judaism* (New York: Schocken Books, 1971), 35–36.

83. For an illuminating discussion of how traditional Jewish conceptions stressing the belief in a supernatural Redemption as the grand finale of the redemptive process can be reconciled with the advocacy of political activism and recognition of the need for human initiative, see Menachem M. Kasher's *Hatekufah Hagedolah*, (Jerusalem: Torah Shelemah Institute, 1968). Especially important is his treatment of the role of the Messiah Ben Joseph, on pp. 112–113, 140, and 502–518.

CONCLUSION

1. For an extensive discussion of the evolution of Cohen's thinking on the relationship between ethics and religion, see William Kluback, *Hermann Cohen: The Challenge of a Religion of Reason,* (Chico, Calif.: Scholars Press, 1984).

2. See Joseph B. Soloveitchik, *Ish ha-Halakhah — Galui Venistar* (Jerusalem: World Zionist Organization, 1979), 180–186.

3. B. Bava Batra 10a.

4. B. Berakhot 25b.

5. B. Kiddushin 21b.

Glossary

Active euthanasia: Measures designed to actually shorten the lives of patients in order to end their suffering.

Act-Morality: Prescriptions of how one ought to act or how one ought to intend to act.

Agent-Morality (Virtue-Ethics): Prescriptions concerning the personality traits one ought to cultivate.

Aggadah: Nonlegal religious teachings.

Amora: A post-Tannaitic Rabbinic authority during the period of the development of the Talmud.

Aveirah Lishmah: A sin committed for the sake of God.

Baraita: Tannaitic teaching not included in the Mishnah.

Chesed: Lovingkindness.

Consequentialism: Ethical theories that evaluate goodness or rightness in terms of the ensuing consequences.

Da'at Torah: Opinions offered by halakhic authorities for guidance on sociopolitical issues. Although there is no legal basis for these opinions, advocates of this conception claim that the sociopolitical intuitions of halakhic scholars are authoritative.

Darkhei Shalom: Rabbinic ordinances that were enacted to promote social harmony. See also "Eivah."

Deontological: An ethics that stresses duty; it revolves around the intrinsic rightness of an act or an intention rather than the ensuing consequences.

Derekh Eretz: Etiquette, manners, socially acceptable conduct, or wordly occupation.

Eivah: Animosity. Various rabbinic ordinances were prompted by the desire to prevent friction.

Emotivism: An ethical theory that states that ethical propositions or statements cannot be true or false, because they are merely designed to express or evoke feelings.

Eruv: Symbolic devices that permit activities on the Sabbath or holidays, which otherwise would have been prohibited by Rabbinic law.

Ethical Monism: The belief that the truth or falsity of all ethical beliefs depends upon a single criterion.

Eudaemonism: An ethics that defines goodness in terms of what is conducive to the happiness of the agent.

Gemara: Discussions of the Mishnah by Amoraim and subsequently edited by Sabbaraim.

Genetic Fallacy: The fallacy of maintaining that one understands the meaning of a phenomenon by reference to its origins.

Halakhah: Jewish religious law.

Intuitionism: An ethical theory maintaining that the truth or falsity of ethical beliefs can only be apprehended by intuition.

Kevod Ha'beriot: Concern for the dignity of human beings.

Mishnah: A compilation of Tannaitic teachings edited by R. Judah the Prince.

Mitzvah: A commandment of God.

Noahide Laws: Laws addressed to all descendants of Noah and therefore applicable to non-Jews as well. They include prohibitions against homicide, theft, adultery, idolatry, and blasphemy, and the obligation to administer justice.

Passive euthanasia: Failure to expend efforts to prolong the lives of terminal patients in order to spare them further suffering.

Prescriptivism: An ethical theory stating that ethical propositions or statements do not describe intrinsic properties of objects or actions but express our beliefs as to how one ought to evaluate them.

Supererogation: Conduct or dispositions that go beyond what is required by duty or obligation.

Talmid Chakham: Torah scholar.

Tanna: A Rabbinic authority during the period when the Mishnah was developed.

Torah Min Hashamayim: The belief that the Written and the Oral Torah are based upon divine Revelation.

Tzedakah: Charity.

Utilitarianism: An ethical theory that states that the consequences in terms of social utility determine the moral propriety of an act or disposition.

Bibliography

My views on the nature of Jewish ethics have evolved over the years. I first formulated some of my ideas in articles and chapters published in various journals and books. My writings that are most relevant to this book are, in chronological order:

"Metahalakhic Propositions." In *The Leo Jung Jubilee Volume,* edited by Menahem M. Kasher, Norman Lamm, and Leonard Rosenfeld, 211–221. New York: Jewish Center, 1962.

"Pluralism and the Halakhah." *Tradition* (Spring 1962): 221–240.

"Covenantal Imperatives." In *Samuel K. Mirsky Memorial Volume,* edited by Gersion Appel, 3–12. New York: Yeshiva University, 1970.

"The Jewish Attitude toward Psychedelic Religion." In *Judaism and Drugs,* edited by Leo Landman, 135–143. New York: Federation of Jewish Philanthropies, 1973.

"Jewish Values and the Crisis of the Family." In *New Directions in the Jewish Family and Community,* edited by Gilbert S. Rosenthal, 31–40. New York: Federation of Jewish Philanthropies, 1974.

"Darkhei Shalom." In *Gesher,* Bridging the Spectrum of Orthodox Jewish Scholarship (a publication of the Students' Organization of Yeshiva Rabbi Isaac Elchanan Theological Seminary, 1978), 80–86.

"Law as the Basis of a Moral Society." *Tradition* (Spring 1981): 42–54.

"The Maimonidean Matrix of Rabbi Joseph B. Soloveitchik's Two-

Tiered Ethics." In *Through the Sound of Many Voices: Writings Contributed on the Occasion of the 70th Birthday of W. Gunther Plaut,* edited by Jonathan V. Plaut, 172–183. Toronto: Lester and Orpen Dennys, 1982.

"Health Care Issues in Jewish Perspective." In *Liturgical Foundations of Social Policy in the Catholic and Jewish Traditions,* edited by Daniel F. Polish and Eugene Fisher, 39–54. Notre Dame: University of Notre Dame Press, 1983.

"Obligations Towards Aged Parents." In *The Jewish Woman in the Middle,* edited by Joseph Lowin. Hadassah Study Series. New York: Hadassah, 1984.

"*Imitatio Dei* in Maimonides' Sefer Hamitzvot and the Mishneh Torah." In *Tradition and Transition: Essays Presented to Chief Rabbi Sir Emanuel Jakobovits to Celebrate Twenty Years in Office,* edited by Jonathan Sacks, 321–324. London: Jews' College Publications, 1986.

"Orthodox Judaism and Human Purpose." *Religion and Human Purpose,* edited by W. Horosz and T. Clements, 105–122. Dortrecht: Martin Nijhoff Publishers, 1986.

"Law, Philosophy and *Imitatio Dei* in Maimonides." *Aquinas* 30 (1987): 27–38.

"Samson Raphael Hirsch's Doctrine of Inner Revelation." In *From Ancient Israel to Modern Judaism: Intellect in Quest of Understanding, Essays in Honor of Marvin Fox,* vol. 4, edited by Jacob Neusner, Ernest S. Frerichs, and Nahum M. Sarna, 3–11. Atlanta: Scholars Press, 1989.

"The Centrality of Virtue-Ethics in Maimonides." In *Of Scholars, Savants, and their Texts: Studies in Philosophy and Religious Thought — Essays in Honor of Arthur Hyman,* edited by Ruth Link-Salinger, 251–260. New York: Peter Lang, 1989.

"The Enlightenment, the Emancipation and the Jewish Religion." *Judaism* (Fall 1989): 399–407.

"Confronting the Challenge of the Values of Modernity." *The Torah U-Madda Journal* 1 (1989), 104–112.

"Foundations of Jewish Ethics." In *The Solomon Goldman Lectures,* vol. 5, 119–127. Chicago: Spertus College of Judaica Press, 1990.

"Nuclear Deterrence and Nuclear War." In *Confronting Omnicide,* edited by Daniel Landis, 224–233. Northvale, N.J.: Jason Aronson, 1991.

"Breuer and Kant." *Tradition* (Winter 1992): 71–76.

Recent Works in General Ethics (Annotated)

Hampshire, Stuart. "Morality and Pessimism." In *Public and Private Morality*, edited by Stuart Hampshire, 1–22. Cambridge: Cambridge University Press, 1978.

A persuasive argument against ethical monism.

MacIntyre, Alasdair. *After Virtue*. Notre Dame: University of Notre Dame Press, 1981.

This book shows that the repudiation of the classical doctrine of virtue has left ethics with no alternatives but emotivism and prescriptivism, which essentially amount to nihilism.

Williams, Bernard. *Ethics and the Limits of Philosophy*. Cambridge, Mass.: Harvard University Press, 1985.

A convincing demonstration that ethics ultimately rests upon intuitions.

Recent Works in Jewish Ethics (Annotated)

Ahad Ha'am. *Nationalism and Jewish Ethics: Basic Writings of Ahad Ha'am*, edited and introduced by Hans Kohn. New York: Schocken Books, 1962.

A widely quoted view that Jewish nationalism is distinguished by commitment to a unique ethics.

Borowitz, Eugene. *Exploring the Covenant*. Detroit: Wayne State University Press, 1990.

A liberal approach to Jewish ethics, which insists that the Covenant conform to the requirements of our autonomous conscience.

Buber, Martin. *The Writings of Martin Buber*, edited by Will Herberg. New York: Meridian Books, 1956.

A useful introduction to one of the most influential Jewish thinkers of our time.

Cohen, Hermann. *Religion of Reason Out of the Sources of Judaism*, translated by S. Kaplan. New York: Frederick Ungar Publishing Co., 1972.

Reason alone can serve as an instrument of Revelation.

Fackenheim, Emil. *Encounters Between Judaism and Modern Philosophy*. New York: Basic Books, 1973.

Of special importance is the chapter "Abraham and the Kantians," in which the author grapples with the issue of how concern with autonomy can be harmonized with Revelation.

Fox, Marvin. *Interpreting Maimonides.* Chicago: University of Chicago Press, 1990.

An invaluable guide to the understanding of Maimonides.

Kluback, William. *Hermann Cohen: The Challenge of a Religion of Reason.* Atlanta: Scholars Press, 1984.

An eminently readable introduction to the philosophy of Hermann Cohen.

Leibowitz, Yeshayahu. *Yahadut, Am Yehudi U'Medinat Yisrael.* Jerusalem: Schocken Books, 1976.

There are no Jewish values. Judaism is reduced to obedience to Halakhic norms.

Lichtenstein, Aharon. "Does Jewish Tradition Recognize an Ethic Independent of Halakha?" In *Modern Jewish Ethics,* edited by Marvin Fox. Columbus: Ohio State University Press, 1975.

A profound analysis of the relationship between Halakhic and ethical norms.

Rotenstreich, Nathan. *Jewish Philosophy in Modern Times.* New York: Holt, Rinehart and Winston, 1968.

An account of the predominant role of ethics in modern Jewish philosophy.

Soloveitchik, Joseph B. *The Lonely Man of Faith.* New York: Doubleday, 1992.

A classic exposition of the thesis that Halakhah calls for both activism and quietism.

———. *Halakhic Man.* Translated from the Hebrew by Lawrence Kaplan. Philadelphia: The Jewish Publication Society, 1983.

This book stresses the pivotal role that Halakhah assigns to human creativity.

Spero, Shubert. *Halakhah, Morality and the Jewish Tradition.* New York and Hoboken: Ktav and Yeshiva University Press, 1983.

A valuable study of the relationship between ethics and Halakhah.

Twersky, Isadore. *Introduction to the Code of Maimonides.* New Haven: Yale University Press, 1980.

Chapter 6 of this volume is indispensable to an understanding of the Maimonidean position on the interaction between Halakhah and ethics.

Index of Names

Index of Subjects

Numbers preceded by *n* or *nn* refer to note(s) on pages cited.

saving of life, *see* life preservation
science, 22, 105, 107
secular ethics, 111, 113, 133*n*1
  halakhic ethics and, 7
  prudential ethics and, 83
  theists and, 16
  welfare rights and, 64
self-alienation, 102
self-defense, 59
self-denial, 55
self-esteem, 84
self-evident propositions, 34, 92
self-idolization, 106
self-interest, 4, 48–52, 58, 88
selfishness, 45–46, 77
self-legislation, 28
selflessness, *see* altruism
self-perfection, *see* perfection
self-preservation, 10, 92, 94, 99
self-surrender, 85, 104, 119*n*51
Seven Laws of Noah, 17, 118*n*46
sexual morality, 111
sexual perversion, 45, 46
sha'atnez, 26, 120*n*70
shalom bayit, 41
Shekhinah, 104
sickness, 55, 60, 104, 126*n*8
Sinaitic Covenant, 9, 29, 117*n*30, 134*n*24
  Abraham and, 14, 117*n*32
  altruism and, 63
  holiness command and, 26
  political aspects of, 93
sin offerings, 126*n*10
sins, 10, 12, 45, 106
  expiation of, 54
  justification of, 30
  quantification of, 131*n*33
  rebuke of, 47, 58
  repentance from, 75
  repression of, 130*n*16
situational ethics, 100
slander, 89
"slave morality," 63
slavery, 34
smoking, 112
social contract, 94, 135*n*51
social conventions, 18
social utility, *see* utilitarianism
social welfare, 40–52, 53, 62, 64

sociopolitical activism, 108
Sodom, 45–46
Spartan morality, 23
spiritual perfection, *see* perfection
spiritual regeneration, 54, 55, 106
spiritual rewards, 42–43, 58–59, 77, 80, 127*n*28, 132*n*47
  from asceticism, 55
  from charity, 56–57
  from suffering, 54, 126*n*8
state authority, 94
state executions, 20, 43
state morality, 36–37, 92, 93, 97
states of mind, 68–70, 71, 74, 75, 81, *see also* character traits; virtuous dispositions
stewardship, 12
subjective intuitions, *see* intuitions
suffering, 10, 53–55, 57, 61
  of dying persons, 90, 91
  of God, 53, 103–4
suicide, 59, 92
supererogatory conduct, 26–27, 79, 82, 114
"suspension of the ethical," 19, 20

ta'amei ha–mitzvot, 16
talmidei chakhamim, 41, 75, 76, *see also* Rabbis
technology, 12, 85, 105, 107, 111
Temple of Jerusalem, 106
Ten Commandments, 69, 96
terminal illnesses, 60
theists, 16
theocentricity, 4, 17, 18, 19
theodicies, 54
theonomy, 33
tikkun ha-olam, 47
tithes, 66
Torah, 9, 26–27, 44, 47, 74, 131*n*44
  on altruism, 46, 48, 49
  angels and, 104, 113
  on animals, 116–17*n*18
  conscience and, 28, 29
  First Commandment and, 69
  human dignity and, 25–26, 59
  human-Divine cooperation in, 102
  on ingratitude, 96
  interpretation of, 7, 116*n*7a